A Thousand Cranes

and Other Stories

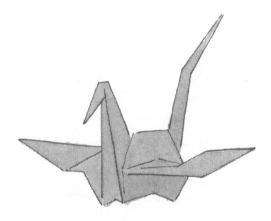

Lee Isaacson Roll

Cantraip
Press

A Thousand Cranes

and Other Stories

Cover design and interior illustrations by Klutch Stanaway
Book interior design by Mary Maddox

Cantraip Press, Ltd.
2317 Saratoga Place
Charleston, Illinois 61920

ISBN 978-0-9844281-6-8

LCCN 2014955942

CONTENTS

II Brasil with an S: a Memoir

FOREWORD

I FIRST MET LEE WHEN she walked into my office at Eastern Illinois University and politely asked whether she could have a word with me. I was used to having words with students, usually younger and much less elegantly dressed ones. I was struck by Lee's confidence and energy in addition, of course, to her stunning good looks: she was tall and thin with golden blond hair and the cheekbones of a model.

We had chatted for almost an hour when she asked whether I'd be willing to be a reader on her thesis committee. She was writing a memoir about the years she'd spent in Brazil, 1969-1971, teaching English at the American School in Rio de Janeiro. Although I sensed Lee's keen intelligence and eloquent ways with words, I was still apprehensive; what if she wasn't a very good writer?

The memoir about Brazil—*Brasil with an S*—turned out to be the best creative writing thesis I'd read in my many years as a college professor. Lee combines her talent for poetry with her bent for self-deprecating humor, adds the ability to tell a good story, and leavens this mixture with a deep understanding of human nature. Her subjects include everything from the ritual dances of the Afro-Brazilian religion called macumba, to the homeless boys of Rio, to meeting with Pulitzer-prize winning poet Elizabeth Bishop. Most of the memoir is included in this book.

I kept in touch with Lee after she defended her thesis. She joined Past~Forward, the community memoir group that Janet Messenger and I started in 2008, and soon became its starring member. She wrote with honesty, insight, and compassion about her children, her travels, her experiences in high school, and her battle with the cancer that eventually took her life. Humor was a hallmark of her writing. "Escapade," about a disastrous family trip to St. Louis, reminds one of an edgy Erma Bombeck. "I Can't Promise to Obey," Lee's account of eloping to Reno, is another classic, revealing an acute awareness of life's absurdities and an abiding love for her husband Jim, affectionately known as JR.

Lee "graduated" from Past~Forward to the Eastern Illinois University Writer Babes, a small group of professional writers and academics who meet every two weeks to critique each others' work for possible publication. The last year and a half before she died, Lee stopped going to most of the organizations and groups she belonged to, but she always tried to make it to the Babes, a sign of her commitment to serious writing. Several of her pieces were published: "I Can't Promise to Obey" in the widely read *Good Men Project*, and "Church" in the literary journal *Bluestem*. Lee was also an astute and encouraging critic of the writing of her peers. I always looked forward to her comments and suggestions.

This book has been a collaborative labor of love. Mary Maddox, owner of Cantraip Press and one of the Writer Babes, oversaw the layout, design, and publication of *A Thousand Cranes and Other Stories*; Writer Babe Angela Vietto proofread the manuscript; I selected the pieces for publication and did some very minor editing; and Klutch

Stanaway, Lee's son-in-law, created the beautiful cover illustration as well as the cranes that grace the inside of the book. We are all indebted to Jim Roll and his lovely family for their support and encouragement of this project.

All proceeds from the book will go to the War Writers' Campaign, a nonprofit independent publisher that serves as a platform for the writing of American veterans. The War Writers' Campaign was started by Ryan Weemer, a friend and former student of Lee's. You can find out more about the organization at http://www.warwriterscampaign.org/.

— Daiva Markelis

I
STORIES AND POEMS

SPECIAL EDUCATION

In rain, at the Special Olympics,
I hold my sobbing daughter,
recall how, years ago,

Chester, a shrub of a man late in his fifties,
shuffled in through Scotch broom
to clean the yards on two sides of our block.
On her doorstep, my grandmother, sharp tongued,
points us toward weeds.

Squat as a fireplug, no bigger than me,
Chester is smiling, pulling my hand,
but I grab at his pocket for candy and gum.
Neighborhood kids call him mongoloid
but love him and squabble over
who'll walk next to him home.

Lee Isaacson Roll

Foreign and flubbing, my fingers
don't know flowers
from weeds. But, from iris and peonies,
Chester shakes ants, squashes mealy bugs, laughs
ear to ear. He prunes roses, picks aphids, and snips away wilt,
cuts cankers, pulls dandelions and clover,
bags the refuse and ties double-loop knots.
Grins and smiles at the job done well.

When the yard is neat, I am off
to hopscotch and red rover. But I hear,
around Chester, laughing, and from grandma,
the warmest of words. And from her pockets
to his hands go nickels and dimes.

Here on my lap, my daughter cries.
Disqualified, she's been sent back,
normal in size, shape, and brain.
Not special enough to laugh
and race with those who win ribbons,
even those who run last.

PERFECTION

I GOT THE DOUBLE WHAMMY when it comes to DNA-induced neurosis. My dad was an accountant, the think-inside-the-box kind who made sure every angle of that box was perfect and every wall was plumb. He kept ledgers balanced to the penny and liked vanilla ice cream. He was a Depression-era farm boy who only knew how to work, not play. I'm fairly certain that the Post Traumatic Stress Disorder that he developed from World War II sifted down onto us kids and even onto his beloved Springer Spaniels. He bit his fingernails until the day his mother died. By the time I was in school, he was the president of a large cooperative plywood plant. His decisions impacted the lives of the families of the several hundred men and women who worked there. How could these people trust my dad's decisions if his own kids weren't the most exemplary examples of good children?

My mother was an artist, an abstract painter. So you'd think she would be the yin to my dad's yang, living either a bohemian life in a gabled loft or twirling through meadows with armloads of daisies.

17

But, no. She had a truckload of down-to-earth issues to deal with, too. She was an only child, and her father, an architect, died when she was just a toddler. From everything I've heard, Mom's mom, my grandma Engdahl, was a sweet, fragile woman whom everyone adored and whom everyone wanted to take care of. From early childhood, Mom was the mom to her mom. When Mom got her first teaching job, she left Salt Lake City and headed for Montana. She took her mother with her. When she got a job at a bank in California, she took her mother with her. After she married my father and had children, her mother lived with us. When Grandma died, a huge irreparable hole was left in Mom's heart. Eventually she went back to teaching.

Champions of causes, both my parents were unyielding in their dedication to upholding social justice. They were against the war in Viet Nam when most folks didn't even know there was a war. They quit the Elks Club as soon as they got wind that only white boys could enter the basketball shooting contest. They knocked on doors to solicit votes for candidates who supported the same left-leaning ideas they believed in. They opened the doors to our home for foreign exchange students, and they traveled the world...Europe, South America, China. They tried, always, to do what was good and honest and true.

So my brain was pretty much hard-wired by nature and nurture for perfectionism. Unfortunately, this perfectionism is often irrational and causes a multitude of stupid, insignificant things to get to me. The napkin that is folded wrong at a place setting. Pencils that aren't sharp. A coffee stain on a blouse. Towels stacked the wrong way.

I feel great guilt if I reread a sent e-mail and find a spelling or punctuation error. I'm still obsessing over the typo in my master's thesis—it should have been "on," not "in," on page 147. One of my daughters has fits because I can't make a less-than-perfect copy on the copy machine. I have to make the first copy, trim the edges, tape it with magic tape with equal margins to a clean piece of paper, and recopy. If there's a smudge, I have to use whiteout and recopy again. These are things that are enough to cause me to lose sleep. You can't even imagine what happens when I have a two-faced lying boss, a student who is nonchalant about plagiarizing, a pastor who is having an affair with a parishioner, or a legislator who is interested first and foremost in lining his own pockets.

When I was in my early twenties, I was given a test by a psychologist. In my forties, I was tested again. Both docs said I was off the charts in ethical behavior. On paper, it sounds good to be ethical, but more often it's a huge burden. I support a 100-pound moral compass around my neck that pulls my muscles and gives me a backache. A friend once put his hands on my shoulders and said, "You don't have to be the conscience of Edgar County."

I see a colleague at school copy the state tests when we are forbidden to make copies. I go to a workshop and an administrator from another district says he politely tells kids who wouldn't score well on the state exams to stay home on test day. It's illegal to smoke on school grounds, but the rules apparently don't apply to our principal, the person who evaluates me. With every cell in my body, I want to throw his cigarette to the ground and stomp on it. Then, of course, because of my perfectionistic tendencies, I would have to sweep up every loose particle of tobacco and dispose of it properly. In my book these are crimes, but a lot of people I know just shrug and say, "What's the big deal? Who cares?"

Yes, the compulsion to do what's right invades every inch of my body. It could be 2 a.m. on a moonlit night. I'm out in the country. I come to a four-way stop. There are no headlights in any direction. I pull up to the sign, stop completely, look right, left, right, and proceed with caution. My son-in-law would sail right on through the stop sign without a thought. I wear my seatbelt when I drive down our lane to pick up the mail. He doesn't wear his seatbelt when he's buzzing up and down the dirt roads on our farm in his pick-up. This lack of obeying the law provides me with a new dilemma. Will my grandkids have a fuzzy vision of right and wrong and end up in jail because their dad runs stop signs at 2 a.m. and doesn't wear his seatbelt?

Once I paid for a bedspread with my credit card. It wasn't until I got home that I realized I'd signed the slip for $9.99 instead of $99.99. In a panic, I called the store. "Are you kidding?" the clerk replied. "Just figure you got a good deal and keep your mouth shut." Obviously, I don't even have to consider what I'd do if I found a wallet full of money. I am almost completely incapable of conceiving that there actually are people who would pocket the cash and run. But there are. And that thought makes me miserable.

And sleepless.

WORDS

I LIVE ON 9TH STREET in the house with the belly-button door-knob. Every other house I know has a regular doorknob on the side, but our doorknob is right in the middle of the green front door like a big round button on a belly. One block north of my house is 8th Street, the street the library is on. My street isn't paved, but 8th is. Both streets end in grassy places—"empty lots," we kids call them—that are mowed once or twice during the summer but mostly are tangled up with wild blackberries and some stinging nettles and thistles blown in from Canada. When I'm a brownie scout in a couple of years, I'll learn the names of lots of plants. I know Queen Anne's Lace, bracken fern, huckleberry, and salal, and already I'm learning the names of some trees.

Most streets in my town end in the air. Because we're on an island. At the end of the street, there's no place to go except down. Both 8th Street and 9th Street drop hundreds of feet to railroad tracks that run along the beach. It's a skinny beach, even at low tide. I've never seen a train on the tracks, and even if a train came chugging along,

21

it couldn't go anywhere because the tracks are broken. Maybe once upon a time, the tracks connected the two salmon canneries that are built on stilts out in the water. Under one of the canneries, we swing out over the waves on a rope. Green waves like muscles roll over the beach and crash on driftwood logs that make splinters when you rub on them too hard.

We kids say 8th Street is made of "cement." (It will be a long time before I know the difference between cement and concrete.) We can bounce a ball straight up and down on 8th Street, ride bikes and draw hopscotch squares with yellow or white chalk. On 8th Street when we fall, our knees look like someone dragged a sharp-toothed comb over our skin. On 9th Street balls bounce every which way, and our scratches and scrapes are black with gravel and it takes a lot of soap and water and the red stuff like fingernail polish — mer cur o … chrome — before our moms say, "You'll live."

Eighth is wide, like what I think a boulevard might be (before I know what a boulevard is). Between the sidewalks and the street, wide branched trees are planted on strips of myrtle, the kind with blue flowers, and some yellow flowers that look like they should grow in Hawaii, not here where it's cold. They stink. The trees are calendar trees, green for June and yellow orange for October. They are trees with good shadows like in books about how to make good photos or paintings with the right kinds of dark and light. Sometimes their roots hump up the sidewalk and crack the cement.

The 8th Street houses are big — two stories with picture windows that look out over Guemes Channel, which is dark green when it's sunny and dark gray when it rains. It's a mile across the water to Guemes Island. For the people on Guemes, their whole life depends on the ferry schedule. Lucky for us, our island has a bridge, so if we go to Seattle, we can come home whenever we want. Some of the houses on 8th Street remind me of the wheelhouses on the tops of ships where the captain is. The houses even have bridges like on ships so people can see the water. There are lots of ships and fishing boats and tug boats on Guemes Channel. Everyone knows that in my town, a view of the water is really important. If your house can see the water, it's worth a lot of money. My house is on the small side, and if my mom has a baby girl, I'll have to share a bedroom, but we can see the water, not as well as the people on 8th Street, but we can see it. People on 8th Street are richer than people who live on 9th Street.

Depending on how you look at things, Louie Dorbolo's house is either the first or the last house on 8th Street, next to the empty lot. Louie is what my mom says is a little "ornery," a word with an r in it that some people say and some people don't.

Mom and I have to pass Louie's to get to the library. I start holding my breath a long time before we get to his house and I count the steps, but I won't hold her hand. Step on a crack, break my mother's back is what I think about. I jump over cracks on purpose, and I hold my breath even though sometimes I think I'm going to turn purple and burst open. (Mom says to say "burst" not "bust.") Finally we get past Louie's house and I can let out all my air.

We walk a few more blocks and we're almost to Bobo's house. Bobo is a baby gorilla, a real live gorilla from Africa who can play the piano and eat with a spoon. He is famous because he was in Life magazine on November 19, 1951. He lives with Claudia who is three years older than me and is really pretty. She plays the record "When the Moon Comes Over the Mountain" by Kate Smith for Bobo because it's his favorite song.

I always hope that Bobo will be outside swinging on his tire, wibbly-wobbling out from the monkey tree in his yard. He wears a diaper and shorts, baby blue shorts with two buttons at the waist for suspenders. Mom says Bobo's in big trouble. He slammed the door to the greenhouse and broke all the glass. I wonder what it means, "People who live in glass houses shouldn't throw stones." Someday Bobo will have to go to Woodland Park Zoo in Seattle where they know what to do with gorillas. But do zoo people know what to do with grown-up gorillas who were raised like little boys?

I remember that once we played ring-around-the-rosy and Bobo scratched me with his fingernail. By accident. His fingernail was yellow and dirty, like an old man's fingernail, an old man who works on old cars in a dirty garage with dirty windows and just a little light coming in like a cone. And spider webs without spiders, just dusty old webs that hang like pieces of skin on chapped lips.

I don't see Bobo anywhere.

We keep walking. Past Janie's house. Past the old hotel that now is just tumble-down brick. No roof, not really even any walls, just piles of broken brick with bushes and trees growing up through the boards that used to be the floors. Once I found a giant diamond under one of the boards. It was as big as a head of lettuce. It was blue green, and see-through. My dad says it isn't a diamond, not even close. He says it's only melted window glass from when the hotel burned down a hundred years ago or after the war. But I decided to keep it on my dresser on a lace doily for a long time, just in case dad doesn't know what he's talking about. My mom likes to dye lace doilies in tea or marigold flowers. And sometimes in red roses. Once she used a doily to make a collar for my dress. She sewed the dress on her sewing machine. The collar was pink from beet juice.

We're getting close to the library. It's a Carnegie library. Mom says there are more than two thousand Carnegie libraries, maybe even three thousand. A man from Scotland, like Jimmy who helped raise her because her daddy died when she was little, gave lots of money to build libraries all over the world, but especially in America and mostly just in countries that speak English. She says Mr. Carnegie liked big doors and really big staircases. Mr. Carnegie also used really big words. She says Mr. Carnegie says that big stairs mean that a person is "el e vated by learning." He also liked lampposts and they mean "en light en ment." My mom is a teacher, and she says I can use big words just like Mr. Carnegie. She's not a reading teacher, but she's an art teacher who reads.

Our library has two lampposts in front of it. The globes on the lamppost are like white milk glass. I know they're like milk glass because my mom has a collection. She has a milk glass hen with a lid for keeping butter in and a vase and a candy dish and some other dishes, but the hen is my favorite so I remember it best. It has nubbies on the lid. On the sides of the huge staircase leading to the huge front doors of the library, there are four cement sitting-down places. If they were in front of art museums, I'm pretty sure there would be lions on them.

The whole library is cement, just like 8th Street, and with grass and trees, it takes up a whole block almost. Sometimes I like to sit with my new checked out books where the lions should be and dangle my legs over the side, spit on a penny and drop it to the sidewalk that goes to the children's library in the basement. Fingers crossed for Mr. Lincoln head's up. Some little kid would love to find a penny.

The steps down to the children's library are outside on the side of the building and are always in the shade because of the big chestnut trees all over that part of the block. I don't like the stairs to the basement much. They're always wet and cold and mossy. Not really slippery or anything, just dark. Maybe that's why I drop pennies. Because they're bright. The stairs don't get swept much, so leaves and sticks make little nests in the corners of the steps. There's a light on the wall over the stairs, but it's dirty and spider-webby.

The door into the kids' library is heavy. Steel. Like an army door, gray-green with a push bar. Too heavy for kids to push. Little kids need their moms to help them open doors.

The library smells funny. Like pine-smell furniture polish and old ladies and moth wings. When I'm six, I'm happy in the library. I look at pictures and ask my mom what the words say. When I'm six, I can check out six books at a time.

The books I like are on the side of the library away from the stairs, the side where the sun sets, the warm side where lots of light comes in, even when it's cloudy, through the tall windows. It's funny to look up at the windows and see the flower garden above my head, but that's what happens in a basement. On nice days when it's not raining, the sun comes in like a shiny arrow and points to the books I like.

I look for the books about the triplets. One set of books is about boy triplets, and one set is about girl triplets. They are blue-eyed towheads. The boys wear blue shorts. The girls, of course, wear dresses most of the time. They like red dresses with big white dots. And yellow shoes. But, sometimes, when the girls go outside, they wear "overall suits"—that's what the book calls their play clothes—that are just like Bobo's with buttons and suspenders. The kids are always in a "predicament," a word I think is pretty funny when I'm six.

There are lots of different books because the triplets have lots of different predicaments. Sometimes they do things like fall into gingerbread batter or splash red paint on their clothes or get lost when they are picking wild strawberries. They learn a lesson and they never do that thing again. The mother in the stories is always understanding.

The triplets are Swedish because they are towheads. My Grandma Isaacson who came from the Old Country says I'm Swedish and someday I'll go to Sweden and eat seven desserts because that's what Swedish people do. Sometimes she takes me to Runeberg, which is a meeting, to see all the Swedish people who live in my town. I'm scared of all the old people who touch my head and talk half in English and half in Swedish. My grandma's friends are there, but they call each other Mr. and Mrs. even though they're best friends, and they sit together in the afternoon and drink coffee and eat skorpa with sugar and cinnamon crusts or ginger pepparkaka and krumkake with whipping cream if it's close to Christmas. The triplets have friends, but they call them by their first names. The girl triplets' names rhyme. Flicka, Ricka, and Dicka. Flicka means "girl" in Swedish. It's pronounced Fleee ka. The boys' names start with S and are funny. Snipp, Snapp, and Snurr. If I were a boy, I'd like to be named Snipp or Snapp or even Bobo, but not Snurr.

When I'm six, I really, really love the library. And when I'm seven, I love the library even more than when I was six.

❧

WHEN I'M EIGHT, I don't need my mom to take me to the library anymore. I can go by myself. I walk down the block from 9th Street to the empty lot on 8th Street. I'm almost to Louie's house, and I'm holding my breath. When I'm eight, I can check out eight books, so I have eight books to return. They aren't very heavy. Only one of the books is about the triplets. I'm too big to read about the triplets, but sometimes I check out a book anyway. In this one, the girl triplets got new red dresses with white collars and their mother said, "Be sure to keep your new dresses clean." But the girls carried firewood, fed chickens, brought potatoes from the cellar, and milked a cow for an old woman they met on the path to the woods who told them they could call her Aunt Helma even though she wasn't their aunt. They also chased a pig. Their dresses got really dirty. And then one triplet tore her dress when she climbed over a fence for a shortcut back home. They thought it was a terrible predicament, but when their mother found out that they were kind to Aunt Helma, she smiled and hugged them. But she said that the next time they helped Aunt Helma, they should wear their overall suits like the ones that make me remember about Bobo.

I can see some boys come up the hill from Louie's backyard. His backyard is steep. They are older boys, some of them more than twelve. They look like the kind of boys who put salt on slugs and tweeze them up with two twigs and stick them in girls' faces. I heard that once some boys fried ants with a magnifying glass and put them in Jill Brown's little sister's mouth and yelled, "Nola eats mouse turds, Nola eats mouse turds." "Turds" is a bad word.

I walk a little faster, but pretty soon I can feel the boys right behind me. I try not to turn around and look, but before I know what's happened, they are making a circle around me and saying bad things, things I can't tell anybody. I can't walk away because they are too close to me and they're big. Their fingernails look like they've been digging for potato bugs and fish worms. They are boys whose names I don't know. They say I have to go to their fort or they'll put dog poop in my hair. But they don't say "poop."

I don't have a choice, I don't. They're pushing me down the hill, but I don't fall. I keep holding my library books and I keep sucking on my bottom lip. At the bottom of the hill, they have a fort. It's by the Himalaya berries that are taller than Louie's dad's carport. The vines are thick and black and have thorns, and I think of Brer Rabbit and the briar patch. And I keep trying to say, "lippity-clippity, clippity-lippity" like they say in the story and I think how Brer Rabbit says he's going to bust, I mean, "burst" the Tar-baby wide open.

The trees are too tall to see Guemes Channel, but I can hear the beach and I think the tide is coming in. The fort is sawhorses and bent-up plywood and tarps and tree branches. An old smelly army blanket is hanging from the limbs and the boys say it's the door. "In," they say and push me under the blanket and push me down with their worm-digging hands.

It's dark inside. The boys must have pulled all the grass up because the floor is just dirt. There are rocks in a circle and the boys sit on them. And I'm in the middle. I'm still holding my library books, all eight of them.

"Are you scared?" one boy says.

Another boy comes close. I can't see his whole face altogether, just parts of it. I won't let myself see all of him at once. And he wiggles his tongue at me and I see his teeth and they are red like Kool-Aid. He has freckles. A thing like dandelion fluff is in his hair. I put my head down and cover my face with the books. They're not heavy. I tell myself to be a bird and tuck my head into my wing and go to sleep.

I can smell the boys. Like dirt and something sour.

One boy says, "You're staying right here until you take your pants off."

Another boy says, "C'mon, girlie, we got something to show you." And he makes a sucky noise.

And somebody says, "You're too stuck-up, that's what's wrong with you. You think you're too good to talk to us," and I remember that's what Brer Rabbit said to the Tar-baby that Brer Fox made for a trick.

I smell their breath and feel warm air around them. But I'm cold. Shivering. And I try to say "lippity-clippity" and I try to think of the triplets. The triplets always get out of predicaments, and their mother always gives them a hug. Someone pokes me with a stick. My eyes are burning and I squeeze them shut.

"You don't go nowhere until you take off your pants."

From down the block, I can hear a car coming.

"Hey, I think it's my mom," says one boy. "Hurry, she said she'd bring home ice cream sandwiches."

"Don't you dare move," a boy says.

The boys crawl out of the fort and I can hear them run up the hill and go away. I sit for a minute or two, listening. Nothing. I can hear the beach, and I can hear a car go by, but I can't hear the boys. I push the blanket away and peek out.

"Get your goddamn head back inside before I . . . ." His face is just an inch from mine. I can't see his whole face, only his mouth. I don't know his name or what street he lives on.

I pull the blanket closed and grab the books to my chest and curl up as tight as I can. I suck on the knuckle of my pointer finger. "Clippity-lippity. Lippity-clippity," I say inside my head. "Be a bird, be a bird. Be a . . . ."

I wait. For a long time. Listening in the dark. Finally I hear voices again. But I don't know whose voice is whose. I can't think where these boys live, on what street. I've seen them before, but I don't know their names.

They are laughing, and then I hear a sound like scratching and swishing. They're unzipping their pants and they're laughing louder and louder and one is saying, "On target! Ready . . . set . . ." Hot pee is making a noise like sizzling on sticks. I can smell it. "Bull's eye!" someone is yelling, and pee is soaking through the army blanket.

"That's gotta be a record. Beat that, morons!"

They're zipping their pants back up, and they're going back up the hill. I can hear them pushing each other and laughing.

I put the books on my lap and put my head on the books and put my hands over my ears until I can't hear them anymore.

I wait for a long time, a really long time, and I keep my head on the books. I try to think of big words and spell them. "Predicament." "Enlightenment." I remember that Mr. Carnegie said, "Let there be light." Even with my hands over my ears, I can hear a dog bark, and I can hear cars go by. Sometimes I think the car is pulling a boat trailer because I can hear loose chains. I try to hear if the tide is going out or coming in.

Finally I take my hands away from my ears and sit up. I touch the blanket. It's wet and it smells, and I feel like I'm going to have a stomach ache. I peek out. There's no one there. It must be late afternoon, that's how the light seems. I can see, sort of, into the next-door neighbor's yard. There's a clothesline, one of those that's a circle like the spokes of an umbrella. There are clothes on the line, clean clothes stuck on the line with clothespins.

I crawl out into the light, but it's really not light but shade and just a little bit of light. I'm holding the books tight, climbing up the hill, stepping onto the sidewalk. Dr. Long is mowing his grass and is waving at me. Rich people live on 8th Street. I wave, sort of, back.

I walk by the empty lot and see that someone left a lawn mower there, but there's no one around. Now I can see my house, the big rhododendron bush and birds pecking away on the lawn and our dog Skipper asleep on the front porch. I see our front door with the belly-button door knob in the middle. I hold my books tight against my chest and start to cry. But just a little. I can't tell anyone about my predicament because my mouth won't make the right words, so it's not my mother's fault that she doesn't hug me when I walk in the door.

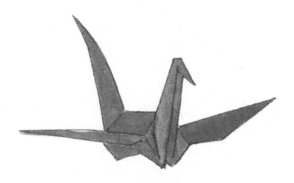

DIVERSITY

MY SON AT THE CIRCUS PUSHES OFF FROM MY THIGHS,
shrieking for ear wings, jigging for Dumbos
rumpled as squash. Under the big top
rolls a pachyderm in pink—
chunky ballerina—a carnie's fat loft.
Lipping bubbles and gum, my daughters, eyes wide,
bounce to the sway, giggle at elephants tied tail to trunk.

Next to us, speechless, my brother's Thai guests,
two tiny girls whose elephant is holy;
shoulder of the world, a cosmos on its back.
Forehead like lightning, straddled by gods,
this colossus careens between monsoons,
over trees, bathing rice in rain.

My children, bobbing, squeal to behemoths
tottering on buckets, huge sniggering jokes.
Stumps for the monkeyshines of midgets and clowns.
My brother's charges, thin as grass,
tight eyed postulants, stiffen like reeds.

CHURCH

Sunday mornings at the Presbyterian Church on Ninth Street I felt empty. In that church basement, painted half beige and half lima bean green, I sat on a folding chair, scuffing and tapping my patent leather shoes against the linoleum, crossing and uncrossing my scabby ankles. My right shoe stuck to my left shoe, making a sound like the smacking of a sloppy kiss. Something was always amiss. My collar was too tight, the elastic on my underpants too loose.

The church basement smelled like an old folks home, like grilled cheese and cold vegetable soup. The air was steamy, damp but cool, and dribbles of wet wiggled down the windows over our heads at street level, inside and out. Our Sunday school teacher told us about sand and wind, flowing robes and turbans, camels and donkeys, dry heat. Growing up near a rainforest, a stone's throw from Puget Sound, I couldn't imagine deserts, couldn't fathom heat waves undulating skyward, mirages, or oases circled with palms.

The teacher's words made no sense to me, so I would squinch my eyes shut and will her to move a step to the right or a step to the left. Then I could see Christ, soft-eyed, hued in golden light, held in by an oak frame. Sometimes, for a millisecond, I could catch a burst of radiance. Then I'd refocus, and Jesus was just head, neck, and shoulders, a yellowish face on browning paper, water-stained from a ceiling leak.

On Sundays, I held a spit-shined quarter to drop into the offering plate to help the helpless and the hopeless: black-skinned kids with runny noses and flies on their faces or yellow-skinned kids with big sores on their eyelids. The teacher passed out color book pictures along with crayons that smelled like old toenails; we were to give life to nomads with curly beards, babies in rushes, babies in mangers. "Don't scribble," the teacher said.

The color book pictures, thick black lines on paper the color of oyster shells, made me bite my lip. The pictures were flat, and I knew that everything had a shadow. The teacher said, "Color the sky blue and the clouds white." But I couldn't. My mother had always encouraged me to make the sky purple or green or any color you can feel: "Look at a blade of grass. See the tiny white stripe? Grass isn't just green. It can be yellow or lavender or blue. Put color on top of color. Don't just use color straight out of the box."

When I was in church, I felt like I was sinning. In our house, color books were banned. In the house of God, I was supposed to follow the teacher's directions and color robes white and sashes brown; in my mom's house, all coats were coats of many colors.

During Sunday school, my lips would quiver. I sucked on the skin between the thumb and the index finger of my left hand until it was red-raw and bleeding, and I bit my ring finger. After headaches and stomachaches created too many skipped Sundays, mom no longer made me go. Dad was fine with it. Whenever he talked about the church, it was with steely eyes and a tight frown. His face would turn blue-black like a storm, and his words would boil in spit, scaring my brother, sister, and me.

Every few years or so, we would rifle through his box of stuff in the closet. Army bars and army patches — 34th Red Bull Division, gold flag-and-eagle buttons, bullet casings, a yellowed copy of the lyrics to "Lilli Marlene," and a handful of tarnished metal pins, one for each year of perfect attendance at the Lutheran church in Rochester where he grew up. We knew better than to ask about the church pins. Once had been enough. He had raged, cursing his own mother for making him go to church every Sunday whether he had a fever or a broken arm or a bee-stung eye.

As I grew older, beaches and woodlands became my sanctuary. Only in nature could I breathe from low down, full and deep, as if air were liquid, silking its way through me. What I knew of spirituality was wet. Rain dropping off juniper quills. The slapping of waves rolling over stones in the moon's tides. A sea bird dipping its wing in water.

On Cypress Island at Eagle Harbor, just off the rocky beach into the dark woods, I built my church. I lashed branches to trunks of trees with hairy twine and lifted armloads of moss onto twigs I had leveled and tied. At first, they were tables and chairs, benches, and shelves. But they grew to be pews and altars, sacred places formed for my kind of worship.

Summer after summer, I returned with my mother and father, sister and brother, to these mossy sanctuaries. Rains misted down, pelted, shivered down, and the moss grew dense and thick. Salal berries clustered thick and purple-black, and bracken ferns unrolled tender new green. I made brooms of fir boughs and swept smooth my squares and rectangles of forest floor. I cut bouquets of the Indian paintbrush and chocolate lilies that grew on the point where the eagles nested and placed them on my piney altars. Each root, leaf, and bud; each feather, each stone was a prayer.

And I knew their names.

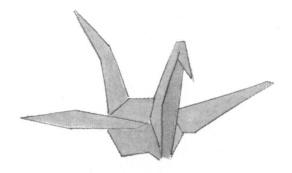

HIGH SCHOOL

WHEN I WAS IN 7th grade, our class was divided into six sections according to test scores. I was a 7-1, one of the smart kids. We got extra attention—Spanish from Miss Hess who had worked on a banana plantation in Costa Rica, field trips, even our own lunch time to receive additional enrichment activities. The 7-2's on down to the 7-6's hated us, but we didn't know that until years later, and since we had each other and teachers who pushed us but also fawned over us, we were happy.

In high school, everyone considered me one of the brains. Not the brain—Galene, hands down, earned that title. I was one of the lesser brains. And I was happy not to be number one, just as I preferred to be vice-president, not president. Galene was valedictorian as expected, and I was salutatorian. I knew that there were kids smarter than I, but I was better at being a teacher pleaser. I was the student who put essays in folders I decorated myself, had neat penmanship, and kept orderly notebooks.

In the spring of our senior year, my status as a lesser brain was confirmed. The top boy and top girl scorers on the SAT were chosen for a three-day science workshop at the ocean. Galene said she'd give up her place so I could spend three days with Mick, the top boy. She wanted Mick and me to be a couple. Galene told the principal that she didn't think she could get away; was there an alternate? Her matchmaking plan ended up being flawed. The second highest girl was Jean Francisco, not me. Galene spent the weekend with Mick. They had long conversations at the beach. Once she even lay with her head in his lap.

Mick had a pattern of breaking my heart. He asked me to the Key Club dance when we were freshmen. He even signed the guest book "Mr. and Mrs." Sophomore year, right after he got his driver's license, he took me to the movies. Because I didn't know any better, I ate garlic bread before the date. I really had no idea how to date. I would think everything was going well, and then he'd ask someone else out the following weekend. Usually someone who was not a brain, someone cute and little. When we were together, he and I had deep discussions—Mick had a lot to do with making me feel like a brain but not like a girl. He wrote in my yearbook "You're too heavy on intelligence for your own good."

Ever since 5th grade, despite Galene's efforts to pair me with Mick, my crush was Greg. It was the kind of crush that gives you shivers and a sick feeling in your stomach, the kind that keeps you awake at night. One summer, probably when we were 6th graders, Greg and I took swimming lessons together at Big Cranberry Lake. I was horrified to see that he could make the bones on the top of his feet stick out like umbrella spokes and ripple them like harp strings. Just as I thought boys who drank orange pop were weird, so were boys who had bony feet. As long as he wore shoes, however, he could still be my crush. He didn't give me the time of day, but he really didn't give any girl the time of day.

In high school, when I walked around the halls with my group of girls, I hoped we'd pass Greg. I hardly ever saw him, but I seemed to run into his older brother, a senior, everywhere I went. He would look at me. I could feel his eyes on me as if he were surveying every inch of my body. I never told anyone that he looked at me. I wasn't even sure that he really was looking. He was popular, president of the student body, a fabulous athlete like Greg, smart, someone who couldn't possibly be interested in me. I told myself I had to be imagining his stares. I looked away and put my head down whenever I saw him coming. I was far too shy to smile.

I had only a couple of dates in high school. I didn't talk to boys much. I felt awkward around them and had no idea what to say. The only boy I wanted to talk to was Greg. In my mind, he was romantic and manly and dedicated to me. In real life, he just passed footballs, shot baskets, and ate ice cream with his cornflakes for breakfast. When he got a full ride to Stanford to play basketball, his attention to sports instead of girls paid off.

Sophomore year, my class elected me as one of the five girls to be voted on by the football team for the homecoming court. When I heard that I was one of the five, I hung my head. I had never even once fantasized about being chosen for a princess of anything. Did I make the list because I was a joke? I wasn't a pimply-faced tub of lard, but never had I thought of myself as anything but a lesser brain, a get-good-grades kind of girl, serious and studious. Only pretty and popular girls got to be princesses. The football boys didn't choose me, and I was relieved. Especially since no one asked me to the dance. After the homecoming game, while everyone else went home to change clothes for the dance, I went home and stayed there.

Junior year I was also one of the five girls on the homecoming ballot. Again the football boys didn't choose me. And again no one asked me to the dance. Senior year was a repeat of sophomore and junior years. One of the five. Not chosen. No date to the dance. And again, I was relieved. Wearing a rhinestone crown, my hair done up in a French twist, wearing dyed-to-match satin shoes, waving from the back of a convertible as it maneuvered around the football field at half-time did not in any way fit my perception of who I was. I didn't think of myself as pretty. Although once, when I was about sixteen, I had walked through my friend Kathie's living room where her father and several other men were drinking cocktails. One of the men said, "Lee Ann, you should be a playboy bunny." I wanted to die, but I also wondered if that grown man had a way of knowing that maybe when I was older I would be pretty.

My high school had a "senior ball," not a prom. Junior year I was in charge of decorations for the ball, an under-the-sea theme; my committee and I were determined to make our ball the most fabulous dance ever. As were most proms and balls during the 60s, the big dance was in the gym. We fashioned a huge clam shell out of chicken wire and Kleenex to shelter the band. We built a pink papier-mâché octopus over the basketball hoop to cover the food tables. Nets and shells and a plethora of sea-themed images hung from the dropped crepe paper ceiling and wound up and down and around the bleachers. We even projected a film of tropical fish swimming over the huge curtain that separated the girls' gym from the boys' gym. I was told later that the dance was a huge success. I had no idea. After 24 hours of decorating, I had fallen asleep on my date's shoulder immediately after we ate dinner, and during the dance, I was too tired to talk. We never had a second date.

When it was time for my senior ball, I was again nominated for the court. Ten girls were elected for the ballot, and of those ten, five would be chosen for royalty: one queen and four princesses. The other five girls would feel honored to make the first cut, but they'd be losers. My friends and several of my teachers said I'd surely win one of the five spots since I'd been one of five for three years running. I started to allow myself to fantasize about what it would be like to be a princess, but I wouldn't even let myself imagine that I'd be queen.

One day in gym, the girls were talking about the ball. I said, "I hope the same people who always win won't." I was saying what nearly every other senior girl was saying. In our class, Sandy or Sandra, both tiny, cute cheerleaders, both always with a boyfriend, almost always represented our class as princesses.

A few days before voting, Sandra's mother called me. She read me the riot act. In her estimation, I, by saying that I hoped different girls would make the senior ball court, had started a campaign to make sure her Sandra would not be voted in, and, furthermore, she was calling everyone she knew to tell them what a mean, despicable person I was. I was stunned. I hadn't really connected what I had said to either Sandra or Sandy. I wasn't thinking; I was simply parroting what most of the other girls were saying. Yet Sandra's mother made it seem that my comment was my personal war against her daughter. She had no vendetta against any of the other girls who had said the same thing, only me. I was not voted onto the court, and neither were Sandra and Sandy.

I was humiliated not so much for losing but because I had caused a mess. I was embarrassed for what I had done to Sandra and Sandy. And I was too scared and shy to apologize. I just wanted to be invisible. To make matters worse, my English teacher left a card on my desk telling me that I should have been on the court. And then the guidance counselor called me into her office, said it was so wrong that I wasn't on the court, and asked me if I wanted to call my mom. What I wanted was for no one to mention the senior ball ever again. I just wanted to be my lesser-brain self with no worries about popularity, dances or boys.

About that time I had finally smiled back at a boy who looked at me as we passed in the hallway. He was making me forget about Greg. Teddy was a junior and had moved to town from southern California. With his sun-streaked hair, tan, and stories of surfing and cruising in convertibles, he was something of an exotic. He had lived in town before, but his family had moved to California where his dad, a doctor, got caught having an affair with a woman not much older than Teddy. Teddy and his mom moved back to town and lived in a tiny apartment with no yard.

Teddy and I walked the halls together at lunchtime and between classes. We talked on the phone and "dragged the gut," the local phrase for driving up and down Commercial Avenue, the main street through town. We never went on a real date like out to dinner or to a movie; we just hung out together. He didn't have a car, so I let him drive my mom's car.

In senior math, I was one of only three girls in a class of twenty boys. Pattie and Fritzi sat in the front of the room, but I sat at the back of the room with some of the boys. A couple of days before the senior ball, Doug turned to me and asked where Teddy and I were eating before the dance. I could feel my face flush and burn. Teddy hadn't asked me to the dance, never even mentioned it. I was hurt that he hadn't asked me, but I comforted myself with the excuse that he couldn't afford to go because of financial complications with the divorce, and he was too embarrassed to tell me.

One of the boys said, "But everyone thinks you're going with Ted. Nobody asked you because of Ted."

Instead of letting the boys know that I was devastated and I wanted to cry, I changed the subject. I didn't want them to know that I was stung with humiliation. I could read their concern for me in their faces. I could see that they were sad for me. But I changed the subject. I didn't want them to console me. That would have further humiliated me.

On the night of the senior ball, I rode around with a group of other dateless girls, not my usual friends because they all had dates. We got out of town as far away as our parents would allow. Just minutes after pulling into the city limits of Oak Harbor, I saw Teddy. He was going into the bowling alley, his arm around a pretty girl with long blonde hair, a freshman girl I actually knew from Girl Scout camp the summer before.

I couldn't say a word, and I hoped the other girls didn't see him. I couldn't bear for them to know my shame.

All through college, I kept my place as a lesser brain. I didn't date, and I tried to keep my mouth shut. I can still, nearly 50 years later, feel the humiliation and shame of high school.

And I still feel more comfortable with books than people.

BATHROOMS

AIVA, OUR MEMOIR GROUP leader, needs a topic. She closes her eyes, sets her fingers to spinning through the pages of one of those "How to Write Like a Pro" guides as if it's a flipbook of a stick figure pole vaulting. She stops, adjusts her reading glasses, and runs her eyes over the words. She laughs. "Yeah, this'll work. 'Bathrooms You Have Known.'"

Movies in my head start flapping in slow motion, like I'm in an accident and my whole life is flashing before me — my whole life in bathrooms. And, believe me, they aren't the bathrooms you'd see in House Beautiful or Architectural Digest. I'm one of those prissy princess types who resides on a higher plain and who retches and feels bile coming up her throat at even the mention of words associated with certain bodily functions. Pee. Bowel movement. Poop. Shit. Big balls — my mom's favorite. So, the bathrooms I am envisioning after Daiva gives the assignment are making me want to roll up like a pillbug and clamp my mouth, eyes, and ears shut. But no matter how hard I try, the images keep obliterating any and all of my attempts to imagine wiggling puppies, daisies, and bluebirds on my shoulder.

Having to use public bathrooms in Italy back when I was a traveling student was almost enough, but not quite, to make me stop eating pizza and drinking wine for days. Two hollowed out footprints in the cement, shoe size 6, with a hole as big as a Crisco lid. And did the women who used the facility before me miss? You bet they did. Now that I'm of a certain age (senior citizen, retired), with two arthritic hips and a crumbling tailbone, I wonder how on earth those old hairy-chinned ladies pulled up their long black skirts, placed their black-laced shoes in the indentations, and squatted. Obviously, many of them weren't successful, which is why remembering Italian public restrooms makes me gag.

I lived in London at the time, and everyone who knows anything about London circa 1968 knows that the Brits used wax paper instead of the soft, colored, sweet-scented bath tissue we used here in the States. Every engagement with the bathroom in the house my roommate and I shared with a University of London professor and his family required much decision-making, especially in February. There was no heat in the bathroom. Sitting on that ice-cold toilet required fortitude and Antarctic survival skills. Would we, could we, cross our legs and hold on a little longer? Absolutely.

We actually had to make a public declaration to the rest of the family when we wanted to schedule a bath, a once-a-week ordeal of dread. A gas heater warmed the bathwater, but we were warned to conserve both gas and water so we ran only a few inches, shampooed, soaped, and rinsed in a matter of minutes. The bathroom was just down the hall, unheated, from our second-story bedroom, also unheated. I slept in the gray wool long johns my mother crammed in my suitcase. "Just in case," she had said. I can only imagine where she found such an odd item of apparel. Probably at Marine Hardware, outfitters for crews of commercial fishermen headed to Alaska. But mom, as usual, was right. By wearing long johns and curling my goose bump of a body around three hot water bottles, I kept from freezing to death.

By the time I turned 21, I'd logged experiences, both good and bad, in countless bathrooms. I knew the pine-scent bite of air in any and all grade school restrooms, and I'd had my share of gas station nightmares. I'd spent eternally long minutes in the outhouse at the Cheneys' summer house in the San Juan Islands. The two-seater, covered with honeysuckle as thick as a haystack, was bee heaven.

In Girl Scouts I had dug and used latrines on mountainsides in the Cascades, but that didn't mean I liked it. I could never get used to the idea that, like dogs and cows, we were using the world as a bathroom. Mind you, this was a time before biodegradable toilet paper. After a childhood of doing business behind trees on serene islands, I was truly grateful when my parents finally traded in the headless 16-foot boat we spent every weekend on for the 28-foot cabin cruiser with a working, running-water head. Swedish relatives sent us a plaque of a boy peeing into a pot that we were to screw to the door. Apparently Swedes, and people of many other cultures, think fountains of peeing boys, often with tiny cherubic wings affixed to their backs, is art.

Of course, I've experienced some nice bathrooms. After college, my first job was teaching English and creative writing at the American School of Rio de Janeiro. The Rio bathroom was fit for a Roman goddess. All mirror and marble and tile. There was a shower at one end. At the other, beneath the window that looked up the jungle-covered mountain to Corcovado, the statue of Christ the Redeemer, was the tub. Thank goodness Jesus's head was turned away, so he wasn't staring down on me in my birthday suit.

Despite the glory of my Rio bathroom, my roommate and I found ourselves in other Brazilian bathrooms that weren't nearly as nice. For example, down south in Curitiba, trying to save a few cruzeiros, we opted for a hotel that cost about the equivalent of fifty-three cents. The rooms were so small a twin bed and a light switch on the wall were the only features. Even the doorknob intruded on the space. Consequently, we each had our own room. As soon as I turned back the sheet on my bed to take a mid-afternoon snooze, I screamed bloody murder, causing Karen to nearly blast though the paper-thin wall that separated us. Spread-eagled on the sheet was a cockroach the size of a book. It was dead. After regaining our composure, we scraped the lifeless body onto a piece of cardboard and headed to the community john to dispose of it. On the door, in Portuguese, a hand-printed sign read "Do not flush toilet paper. Dispose in wastebasket." It was far too obvious that dozens of hotel residents had used the facility and no maid service had been around for a week or two.

Putting our heads together, we decided to go to the bus station directly facing our hotel. How bad could its restroom be compared to the hotel's sorry excuse? Balancing the corpse on its funereal bier, we crossed the street, pulled open the doors under the girl-in-the-skirt icon and smiled at our contentment. The restroom was reasonably clean, only a few misguided paper towels on the floor and a smudge or two on the mirror. It wouldn't be too much of a challenge to simply walk across the street from the hotel whenever we had the urge. Even brushing our teeth and washing our face would be acceptable in this place. Several stalls were occupied, and we could hear some whispering. The murmuring was followed by some sharp words and then some swearing. Suddenly, from under the door of a stall shot two feet, and a blood-curdling scream pierced our ears wide open. The door flew open, and we raced to the source. There, lying on the floor, clawing at the base of the toilet was a young woman giving birth. Two other women were crammed into the stall with her, sopping up the blood running down her legs and pooling on the tile. The toilet was red with blood and toilet paper.

We left.

DAY ON MULL

THE STORY OF MY day on the Isle of Mull is a test not unlike the pilot's experiment in Antoine de Saint Exupéry's novella *The Little Prince*. When the pilot was a child, he drew a picture of a boa constrictor swallowing an elephant. When grownups saw the picture, they said, "That's a hat." Not a single grownup could see the elephant inside the boa constrictor. The little prince, however, could see into things. He understood what was and what wasn't. He saw the elephant immediately.

Whenever I tell someone about the Isle of Mull, I watch for a reaction. I listen for the response. If he or she makes a face like a prune and says, "Beware of Lambs? That's dumb," I put him or her in the category of "bridge, golf, politics, and neckties" like the grownups in the novella. But if he or she becomes dreamy, smiles, nods, and murmurs, "lovely, just lovely," he or she is put in another category, a very special friend place. This is a person with a heart.

June 26, 1967

THE FERRY SLIPPED OUT into the foggy silence of the Firth of Lorne. In the mist, standing on the top deck, we could make out the shapes of two fingers of land in the distance, one to our right and one to our left. Fog insulated us, muffling all sound, though once I thought I heard a bird, or maybe a child, crying on the shore. White foam folded back over green waves, and the drone of the engine, both monotonous and comforting, reminded me of countless summer days trolling the waters of Puget Sound, my dad at the helm, on my family's boat.

Gulls, lazy in the air, sailed down to the rails and were whipped back on an updraft, thrust high and away. Before us, sea and sky merged into a gray curtain. We were cold. Soon the curtain began to dissolve into a thin veil. In the distance, we could make out some sort of structure evolving in the mist. A castle. And like so many other Scottish castles, it was dark, gray, and cold. By the time we reached the dock, the fog had lifted, and the sun was beginning to shine. The village of Craignure on the Isle of Mull was cast in a golden spotlight spooling down from the heavens.

We could see an old man, small and wiry, his back bent, pacing on the walkway above the wharf, his head moving from side to side and his fingers rubbing his cheek and his chin. When he spotted us, he stood up straight and rushed toward us.

"Aye, Diane, I be Mr. Black, your cousin, come to fetch you." Diane and I, sophomores at the University of Washington, were studying British history in London. Before she left Seattle, she had promised her family that she would find her Scottish relatives. We had stayed with the McNeills in Edinburgh, and now we were to meet descendants of the Clan Maclaine of Lochbuie, Isle of Mull.

Mr. Black helped Diane into the passenger seat and me into the back of the small vehicle, a cross between a car and a panel truck. Where I sat there were no windows. He apologized because I wouldn't be able to see much of the scenery as he drove us over the island to Lochbuie where Diane's other relatives were waiting. The road was one lane, unpaved. We jostled along, rocks scraping the bottom of the truck and clumps of thick grass sending us lurching to one side of the road or the other. He was in a hurry, and the truck grumbled and shook as he shifted from gear to gear. Frequently he pounded on the horn and waved his fist out the open window. Black-faced sheep, dingy as floor mops, trotted off up the treeless hillsides, through flowerless golden-brown heather. Tufts of wool, like cotton bolls, hung from bushes and wisped over bracken ferns. There were no fences. We passed two or three cottages, but there was very little sign of habitation along the road.

Eventually Mr. Black pulled to a stop on a hilltop and pointed out a building, small, but tidy and well-kept.

"That is our school," he said. "But there are no children on this end of the island."

We came to the top of another hill, and he directed us to follow him. Beside a smooth stone about the size of a breadbox, he stopped.

"Kneel here, lassies, kiss the stone and make you a wish."

We did as we were told. I wished, simply, for a good day.

"Now look below to Lochbuie."

Down the hill was a small cove with a pebble beach washed by gentle ribbons of slow-moving waves. Beyond the bay was choppy water, tipped with whitecaps. A broken castle, three stories high with a parapet, stood on the shore. A short distance away were several tiny cottages made of wood and rock, each with garden plots of vegetables and flowers.

"This," he said to Diane, "is the home of your ancestors, the Maclaines. We are called by other names now, but all of us here are Maclaine deep and through."

He drove down the steep hill and stopped at the first cottage. Standing at the door was a stocky man, red-cheeked and smiling. He introduced himself as Roderick, cheerily waved our driver off, and invited us into Marion Cottage. I had to duck to get through the doorway. Inside we met Dorothy.

"Latha math. Ciamar a tha sibh?" Diane repeated the Gaelic greeting she had memorized.

Roderick grinned, laughed out loud, threw open his arms, and scooped Diane to his broad chest. He might even have blinked back a tear. From her chair, Dorothy, although she appeared to be in her mid-sixties, smiled and her eyes lit up with the innocence of a young girl. Arthritic, her body was bent in impossible contortions. Her fingers were so twisted and gnarled they resembled roots, not hands. Her knuckles bulged, and the tips of her fingers splayed in different directions. She would be incapable of brushing her own hair, hooking an eye, or buttoning a blouse. At her feet were Prince-the-Dog and a sixteen-year-old cat they had never named. Lumps of coal burned in the tiny fireplace.

Roderick served Diane and me warm gingerbread on bone china plates and tea in dainty cups. Then he stirred tea, steamed milk, and sugar in a plastic cup, gently wrapped one of Dorothy's hands around it and placed the other hand at the bottom for balance. He kept his hand under hers, and, shaking slightly, she raised the glass to her lips and sipped. I wondered if I had ever seen such a tender moment before. The four of us sat close to the fire, our laps and knees warming at the hearth.

"Never been farther than Oban," he said. "Lived in Lochbuie all my sixty-five years, and there's enough right here to keep me busy another sixty-five." He looked at Dorothy, and she smiled back. "The day is coming that we'll have electricity," he said, "and I'm preparing ourselves for it."

Full of pride, he showed us a supply of nuts, bolts, wires and outlets. Until then, because I was warm and because light spilled into the room through shining windows, I hadn't realized that we were in a home without electricity. We learned that water was pumped from a well, that there was no bathtub, that food was delivered by a truck from the mainland every other week.

Roderick removed our dishes and said that as much as he'd like for us to stay all day, he and Dorothy didn't want to upset the other relatives by keeping us too long. We were expected at each of their houses, and we had to be back in Craignure in time for the last ferry to the mainland.

At the next cottage, I had to duck again. There we met cousins Cathie Currie and Isabel Smart. The house was so small that when the four of us sat in the living room, there was no room for anyone else. It was obvious why we had to go from home to home. No house had a room large enough for all of us. Isabel, her eyes wide, leaned toward us and almost whispered, as if it were a conspiracy, "Tell me, dears, is it true that American cars have windows that go up and down at the push of a button?"

When we told her that what she'd heard was true, she shook her head. "Oh, me, what will they think of next?"

"And," Cathie said. "What about Tini? Oh, that Tini, she had her head so full of ideas. How is she?"

"Tini?" Diane asked.

"Surely you know Tini. Christina? Pretty girl. Such a wave to her hair."

"Sorry, I don't know her."

"But Tini left Mull … remember, Isabel, she left that spring when it was so cold we thought summer would never come. She has lived in Florida for years. You must know her."

Slowly we began to understand. Roderick, who had been to Oban, was the only "experienced" traveler among them. None of them had the slightest idea of the size of the United States. Just as they knew everyone on this end of the island, they assumed we knew every single person in the US. There was no TV here. No movie theater. Not even a radio.

The third cottage was even smaller than the preceding two. We were told by Isabel and Cathie that it was several hundred years old. No one seemed to know how many hundreds of years old, but Maclaines had lived in it for centuries. Now the Black sisters lived there. Both were Misses, never married. We listened as Isabel and Cathie remembered Angus who kept sheep and was a drinker, Lachlainn who married Sarah from Iona and fathered thirteen children. Recalling the past, they all but forgot about Diane and me.

"Oh, never mind, you don't have any idea who these people are anyway. Neither do I, really," Cathie laughed and knocked on the door of the third cottage.

"A moment," said Isabel, and she returned to her house. I watched as she cleared the doorway without lowering her head. Estimating that the opening was about five and a half feet high at most, I wondered how tall—or, more accurately, how short—people had been when the cottage was built hundreds of years ago. Isabel returned, holding two dishes in her hands. Small berry bowls, identical, hand painted with full-blown purple-red roses and gold edging. She gave one to Diane and one to me.

"So you remember Lochbuie," she said, her head tipped, smiling.

In the parlor of the third cottage, sitting next to the coal-burning hearth, we met the Black sisters. They looked nothing like sisters. Both seemed to be in their sixties. The younger was tall and thin. She wore thick glasses and little-girl shoes—Mary Janes with straps that buckled over the tops of her long, thin feet. The older was short and plump. One eye was closed. I wondered if she had lost it or if she'd had a stroke. Her cheeks looked soft and hung like half-filled flour sacks. Both wore flat-fronted black dresses. When I first saw them, I thought of a broom and a bucket. Their cottage, warm and moist, smelled like talcum powder and starch.

After tea, they took us out into the garden, moving aside stalks to show us the buds of flowers. Miss Black the Younger pinched lettuce leaves for us to taste and Miss Black the Older gathered a nosegay of nasturtiums, sweet peas, and yellow pansies for each of us. After brushing dirt and lettuce from her hands, Miss Black the Younger pointed toward the beach. The tide was going out, leaving a marsh of sea grasses and mud, and I could smell salt and fish. Stones from the castle had tumbled onto the shore and into the shallow bay. What was left of the castle loomed dark against a band of yellow light on the bright horizon.

"Walk there, down to Moy Castle before leaving us. The rhododendrons are past their loveliest. We would walk with you, but we're not so able any more to cross rough ground. Sister has a bad leg, and my hips give out. But, first, spend some minutes with Mr. Black before he drives you back to Craignure."

At his house, the last house in the village, we sat before a huge wood-burning stove with doors of all sizes in the front and steaming pots on the top. He repeated what the Black sisters had said: "Go on down to Moy." He told us that the castle had been built in the fifteenth century by Hector of Clan MacLean who, to separate himself from his brother Lachlan MacLean of Duart, changed his name to MacLaine of Lochbuie.

The castle was constructed of beach boulders, large blocks of slate slabs, and schist quarried from nearby Laggan. The walls varied in thickness from one to more than three meters. In some centuries, Mr. Black told us, the Duart Clan and the Lochbuie Clan fought side by side. In other centuries, they fought to the death against one another. One chief made a fortune in Java; another lost the estate and sold it to the English.

"Now the castle is in ruin, such a shame, its walls tumbling down. Look to the center of the ground floor," he said. "There's a fresh water well that has not ever run dry. Run along and come back in time to get ourselves to the ferry."

Diane touched Mr. Black on the shoulder. "Could we leave a little early? My grandma said that if I could, I should go to the inn at Craignure and look at the window in the corner. Would that be too much trouble?"

"No trouble. Allow some extra minutes then. Be back in half hour or so?"

We walked slowly down to the castle, listening to the waves and the gulls, feeling a slight chill in the wind. Rhododendrons, not bushes like those we knew at home, but as tall as trees, grew up around the castle and down to the beach. At first, I couldn't understand how it was possible, but blue irises poked up through the pebbles and out of the salt flats. Then I noticed that the irises had sent down bulbs and roots alongside the narrow fresh water stream that curled around and into the castle and out to the bay.

Moss covered the damp outer walls and vines grew out of the crevices between stones. I touched the walls. Five-hundred-year-old walls. We looked up to the third-story windows and to small square openings that may have been portals for bows and arrows and later for guns. Looking into the doorway of the castle, we saw that rocks had loosened from the sidewalls and that high tides had washed pebbles and driftwood into the first-floor chambers. Wind whistled in the turrets, and we heard a cuckoo bird sing.

We walked back to the cottages, silent. A woman carrying a basket of wildflowers passed by and nodded to us. When we arrived at his porch, Mr. Black asked, "Good outing?"

We told him about the rhododendrons, tall as trees that were like none we had ever seen before, about the irises that seemed to grow in the sea, about the stream and the cuckoo.

"A cuckoo? Where were you standing? On grass?"

"Yes."

"Good. Is there money in your pocket?"

"Not our pockets. Our backpacks."

"Good enough. Hearing the cuckoo when you stand on grass with money in your pocket is an omen. Of good fortune. We'll just say your packboards are as good as pockets. The cuckoo, was he to your right?"

We nodded. "Ah, good luck for a year!"

"When a boy hears a cuckoo, he should take off his shoe. If he finds a hair in his shoe, whatever color the hair is will be the color of his bride's hair. If a girl hears a cuckoo, she should count the notes in the cuckoo's song. The number of notes will tell her how many years until she will marry." We promised him that the next time we heard a cuckoo, we would count.

"Come now, into the car with you."

He drove a short distance, pulled over at the crest of a hill, and led us down a grassy slope on a worn cow path to a valley. In the hollow of the valley was a spring. "Not so muddy that we need Wellingtons," he said. He took two small bottles from his pocket and twisted off the lids. "Fill them bottles. For your daddies. Have 'em drink whiskey with this water. Fine whiskey—well, any whiskey—should be drunk only with water from Mull. And you, lassies, you cannot leave the island without drinking some yourselves."

We knelt down, filled the berry bowls that Isabel had given us with water, and drank. When I dried mine with the hem of my shirt, I read on the bottom, "Made in Czechoslovakia." Isabel must have thought that these bowls, the souvenirs of our journey to Mull, made in a far-off land, were perfect for us.

Diane and I each threw a penny into the pool and climbed back up the hill. At the top, I noticed a small sign, no more than a foot tall, stuck in the ground. Hand-painted in blue on the rough board were the words, "Beware of Lambs." I sat down in the grass, rested my head on my knees and didn't know whether to laugh or cry. We had left London, exhausted from noise, soot, and hurrying crowds. We worried about Vietnam daily. Would my brother have to go? Diane's brother was a Marine in the Middle East. Where would he end up? We worried about civil rights and riots in the South. We studied hard and fretted about grades. But on the Isle of Mull, we needed only to "Beware of Lambs."

With our bowls and our bottles in our pockets, we arrived back at Craignure.

"The inn at the wharf?" Diane asked.

"It's not opened yet this evening, but I'll see what we can do, lass," said Mr. Black.

He left us at the dock, returning a few minutes later with a plump, smiling woman carrying a keychain. She rattled the key in the lock and opened the door.

The pub was cozy—heavy wood tables and a huge stone fireplace.

"Grandma said to go to the table in the corner where the windows meet." Some of the glass in the small panes was clear and new, but most panes were old, so old and wavy that the view outside was distorted, as if we were looking at trees and buildings through water. Diane smoothed her fingers along several of the old panes.

She stopped. "Here it is," she said. "Look. Feel it."

There, scratched into the glass was a signature.

"J.C. Currie. Just like Grandma said. James Currie, my great grandfather."

The proprietress went over to the bar, pulled a bottle off the shelf, and poured four jiggers of Drambuie. She swirled each glass, coating the sides with honey-colored liquor.

"Raise your glasses," she said. "May the Lord keep you in His hand, and never close his fist too tight on you!"

She handed Diane two pieces of paper and pencil. "Make a rubbing to carry home to your grandmother and one to keep."

Diane positioned the paper over the signature and scribbled the pencil over the scratches. The lines and curves of her great grandfather's signature emerged. Carefully she folded the slips of paper and tucked them into the journal she kept in her backpack.

"Hurry, time for the ferry," Mr. Black said.

We ran down the ramp to the deck. We leaned into the railing at the stern and looked back toward Mull as the crewmen threw the heavy lines from the boat to the dock and signaled the captain to set sail. The engines roared, and seawater churned out from the props in deep green whorls. We pulled away. When we could make out only the faintest image of the island, we walked to the bow, faces to the wind. "Beware of lambs," we whispered.

I Can't Promise to Obey

J R PICKED ME UP at my apartment in the dark, and we got to Sea-Tac in the graying pre-dawn. In the fluorescent light of the airport, I could finally see him. Sporting a brand new haircut. And it was too short. What was I doing eloping with this man whose hair was too short? He was probably thinking, "What on earth am I doing, marrying this woman who fed me black cod and seaweed the first time she cooked for me?"

We landed in Reno and were met by my boss, Ronald English, and his wife, Mary Jo. During the summer, I was a receptionist at Dick Balch Chevrolet. For his TV ads, Dick wore a black devil suit and bashed in the headlights, windshields, and bumpers of brand-new Corvettes with a twelve-pound sledge hammer. Through his six-inch Fu Manchu mustache, he sneered, "If you can't trust your car dealer, who can you trust?" Sixty salesmen worked for Dick, and 58 of them were liars, cheats, and philanderers. Although I couldn't trust the salesmen, I could still trust Ronald, the business manager.

When I told Ronald that JR and I—just the two of us—were

eloping, he said, "Well, hold your horses. That just won't do."

He and Mary Jo arrived in Reno a day ahead of us. They had collected brochures from every chapel in town. There was a white chapel, a pink chapel, a blue chapel. Pick any color of a pastel rainbow and there was a chapel. Veils, plastic flower bouquets, and color-coordinated Bibles were all part of the package. The wedding couple could choose music from a box of cassette tapes, and for an extra charge, the tape was theirs to keep. We could also opt for a courthouse and Justice of the Peace for only twenty-five bucks. We went with cheap.

"Get yourselves to the right line," Ronald said. "Quickie marriage, not quickie divorce."

Two couples were in front of us. At the head of the line were two kids, barely sixteen. The guy was chewing hard on a toothpick, and the girl kept her head down and sucked on her lower lip. Her arms and legs were skinny, but her belly stuck out like a beach ball. She must have been about seven months along. A yellow rose was bobby-pinned into her long blond hair, and she was wearing a yellow polyester prom-like dress with a white lace overlay. About six inches of the empire waist had ripped open, and she was trying to hold the fabric over her breast with one hand while signing the papers with the other. She looked terrified, like any minute her daddy was going to bust through the door and shoot them both. The boy was dressed in a blue church suit, a size too small. The pants weren't long enough to cover his white gym socks. He looked terrified, too.

At first, I thought the other couple immediately in front of us was an old man and his daughter. Except that this was the marriage license line, and that kind of relationship was against the law, even in Reno. Hunched over, the old guy obviously needed a walker. He tottered along, hanging onto the elbow of his fiancée. He was ancient. Ninety wasn't a stretch. The fiancée was some thirty years younger. Her fried red hair was teased into a beehive on top and rolled into a French twist in back. The roots were mousy grayish brown, and random strands of hair screwed out of her head like rusted steel wool. Her hair looked hard, like petrified cotton candy.

Finally it was our turn. We showed our birth certificates and our Washington State driver's licenses, answered questions, signed the papers, and headed across the hall to the Justice of the Peace.

The four of us entered the office, and JR was given a number, shoe store style. We sat in metal folding chairs and waited. JR and I sat close with our knees and thighs touching. He, in his tan, gold, and forest green, super-sized, hounds-tooth-checked polyester sport coat, white polyester shirt with green fleurs de lis, striped tie, and gold polyester pants. I, in white bellbottoms and jacket.

A WEEK BEFORE THE trip, Ronald had sent us to his favorite clothes store to see his favorite fashion expert. Her mission was to get JR out of Levi button fly jeans and Red Wing boots into something more Gentlemen's Quarterly-like. JR told the expert that he wanted to wear something green. He chose the jacket. I thought it was ugly, really ugly, but I didn't tell him. The clerk assured us that it was "in"; it was also the only article of clothing in the entire store that had anything much to do with green. She also assured us that mixing checks, stripes, and prints was really "in," definitely the way to go.

I wore all white except for the tiny pink rosebuds in the pattern of the eyelet jacket. My mother had always said that when I got married, she'd make me a wedding dress of white eyelet with ribbons laced through the holes. Instead of her idea of my dream wedding, I was getting married wearing pants made by my roommate, and mom wasn't even going to be at the ceremony. In fact, no one from our families was going to attend.

It wasn't on purpose that we'd chosen a date when our parents couldn't attend; it was just a naïve, lackadaisical approach to scheduling. Somewhat stupidly, we planned the elopement to Reno for a time that worked for us, but not for our families. My mom and dad were going to Europe, and JR's mom and dad had crops to plant on their farm in Illinois.

In the place of a veil, I wore a hat. I loved my hat, white felt with a scalloped brim and cut-out flower petal shapes. I pinned a bunch of fake violets to the tiny white purse I had tucked under my arm because my sister, mom, and I had always given each other real violets for special occasions — and sometimes, for no reason at all.

A sleepy-eyed matron called our number, and the four of us single-filed into the chambers. The office was small and smelled of Pine-Sol. There were no windows. The woodwork was dark from layers and layers of varnish, and the alternating squares of green and beige linoleum had faded, and, in some places, worn through to the subfloor. Fluorescent tube lights glared as in a jailhouse interrogation room. JR's hair looked even shorter, and his jacket looked even uglier.

The JP stood in front of a gray metal desk. He welcomed us, turned to the desk, took a sip of coffee, turned back to us, peered over his glasses, and asked, "Will this be a double-ring, single-ring, or no-ring-at-all ceremony?"

"Single ring," JR said. He'd heard stories of guys who got their ring stuck in the gears of motorcycles or Ford pickups and had to have their whole finger cut off.

The Justice of the Peace licked his index finger and flipped through a loose-leaf, three-ring binder. "Here it is, ring for the bride only. Repeat after me, sir. I, state your full name, take ..."

"Wait," I interrupted. "Wait! You're not going to say 'love, honor, and obey,' are you? I can't say 'obey'!"

He smiled and turned the page. "To have and to hold, to love and to cherish ..."

Before I knew it, the wedding ring was on my finger next to my emerald engagement ring, and the JP was saying, "By the power vested in me by the State of Nevada, I now pronounce you husband and wife."

I left the room first. I heard the JP saying something. I turned, prac-

tically knocking JR over.

"What? What did you say?"

The JP cocked his head, smiled at me, and said, "My blessings once again."

"Oh," I said. "I thought you said, 'Come again', and, believe me, I'm never coming here again!"

And, so far, I've never been back.

ESCAPADE

JR AND I HAD his folks lined up to keep Marcus, our 19-month-old, for a couple of days. No way would he be able to lock step with us and his two big sisters as we carried out The Escapade of Fun and Educational Entertainment we had planned for our girls, Jaime, seven, and Ann, five. Ann had recently let us know that because she was going to "real" school, not Mrs. Jean's pre-school, she was no longer "Annie," but "Ann." (As a side note, 28 years later, when she was pregnant with a baby girl, we asked her what the baby's name would be. She responded, "A name worthy of being the CEO of a large corporation.")

We waved goodbye to Grandma Jacky, Grandpa Bill, and Marcus, and set off for St. Louis-and-Beyond in our fake-wood-sided diesel Oldsmobile station wagon. We were positive we'd fare better than our practice road trip a few months before. For the practice trip, we explained to the kids that we would see how far we could drive before one of them started pinching or poking a sibling. Or panicking because she needed to go to the potty. Or asked the inevitable question: "Are we there yet?" Two miles into the trip, Ann insist-ed she had gone to the bathroom before we left home. Not so. Four miles into the trip, Marcus was screaming because a fly landed on his knee, and six miles into the trip, Jaime was bored. We made it all the way to Oakland. Eight miles away.

Ever optimistic, JR and I were sure that we had planned the per-fect "before school" vacation for the girls. As a teacher, I knew that sometimes just removing one kid from class was enough to positive-ly change the entire chemistry of the class. As a mom, I knew that three kids was the perfect recipe for a "two against one" war. Leaving Marcus at home with plenty of grandparent attention and taking the two girls with us for plenty of parental attention would surely put us in the "win" column for awesome road trip vacations.

Off we went. Three hours later, except for the usual "I'm hungry, I'm starving, I'm thirsty, I'm too hot, too cold, I'm really, really starving, my Pixie Stix, ooooh, noooo, spilled all over my Strawberry Shortcake shirt," the trip was uneventful. We pulled into the parking lot of Six Flags Over Mid-America, ready to whoop up the day.

I had never been to an amusement park before, but, as a kid, and like every other kid in America in the 1950s, I dreamed of going to Disneyland. I watched the Mickey Mouse Club every day after school, and I watched Walt Disney Presents every Sunday night. Deep down I knew that if only I could get to Disneyland, my life would be com-plete. Glitter bombs of fairy dust would explode; the most handsome prince ever would gallop up on his white horse; and all would be right with the world. But despite relentless begging, my dad vetoed trips to Disneyland and all other amusement parks. Too much traffic. Too many people. Plus, he thought Californians were a bunch of weirdo nut cases, and so was anybody else who, on purpose, would go to California. When I pleaded with him, insisting that everybody was going to Disneyland, he said, "By 'everybody,' you mean Kathie and Steve Long. Their grand-parents live a half hour from Disneyland. They don't count."

My kids would not have to beg. I'd present Six Flags to them on a silver platter even before they asked to go. And someday, I'd say "Yes!" to Disneyland and Disney World and whatever other tantalizing "Magical Kingdom" called out to them.

By the time we entered the park, the temperature was rising, but we were from Illinois and used to sidewalk-egg-frying weather. Thrilled by the flashing lights and the circus of sounds, the girls took off running toward the Screamin' Eagle. They had seen it on TV.

"It's the tallest and the longest and the fastest roller coaster in the whole wide world!" Jaime shouted, her red hair flying and her bird legs churning.

We took our place in line behind the other eager Eagle rider wannabes. We got closer and closer to the entrance. The temperature was still rising, but nothing, not even temperatures over 100, could keep us from our destination. Then it came to us. There were no little kids in line. Only big kids. And grown-ups. JR volunteered for Recon. When he returned, sweat was pooling on his neck.

"Height restriction. 42 inches. The girls are too short."

And so it went. Deflated, but determined, we forged on, propping the girls against the measuring sticks, sighing, regretting, moving on. Ride after ride. The girls were just too dang short. And we were getting hotter and hotter. Then we saw it. The Log Flume. No height restriction. Spumes of cool water shot into the air from the bullet-like logs cutting through white water rapids. Laughing, screaming riders plowed through diaphanous rainbows of spray. We also saw a problem, a big problem. In front of us were hundreds of people. Hundreds of hot cranky parents. Hundreds of hot cranky kids.

We pleaded with the girls. "It will be at least two hours before it's our turn. And it's so hot, and there's like only two trees for shade. We're going to cook, kiddos. Let's just keep looking."

"Noooooooo," the girls cried. "We have to ride the logs."

Our estimate of wait time was clairvoyantly accurate. Two hours.

71

The girls drew designs with sticks in the dirt. They made pyramids of pebbles and pine needles. JR made trips to the snack bar to pick up over-priced, watered-down lemon shake-ups. The sun beat down; sweat collected in our armpits and behind our knees. But we were bound and determined to do this thing. We would ride the Flume, come hell or high water.

Finally the family in front of us boarded their log. Our log slammed into the dock, and the college kid "lumber jack" held out his hand to help guide us into position to sit toboggan style. Just as he reached toward Ann, she screamed in bloody terror, tears streaming down her dirty cheeks.

"Noooooo, I won't go, don't make me go, nooooooo ..."

Damn. Another Chuck E. Cheese moment. On her third birthday, when she was still "Annie," we had driven two hours to Springfield in January ice and snow so that we could present her with the pre-eminent kid heaven birthday. When she got to the door, she froze. In front of her was the bigger-than-life robotic Rock-afire Explosion band. Fatz Geronimo the gorilla pounded on the keyboard, his monster-sized black head and wild red eyes pulsing to the music. Billy Bob Brockali the bear opened and closed his huge salivating tooth-filled mouth and beat on the bass while Mitzi Mozzarella the mouse gyrated, wiggled, and screeched out high notes that split our eardrums. Ann was freaked out. Totally. Tears spilled, knees knocked, and her whole body shook. She sobbed and sniffed back tears, wiped her runny nose with the back of her hand, and whimpered. Then she planted her feet and refused to cross the threshold into the dining room. We ordered pizza, begged her to join us, ate the pizza, begged her to join us again, finished the pizza, sang "Happy Birthday" from across the room, picked her up, and left. Her third birthday—kid hell in a nutshell.

It seemed obvious that now, here at Six Flags, after waiting two hours for the log flume ride, we were having another Chuck E. Cheese moment. JR yanked her up around his waist, her arms flailing in front and her legs kicking every which way behind. She was screaming and trying to claw her way out of his grasp. He forced her into the log, holding her wrists while I pushed down on her shoulders. Finally, she was in place. Jaime got in, without a word. I was afraid to look at anyone waiting in line. I was afraid that DCFS agents would leap out from behind the trees, slap handcuffs on us, and haul us away. I knew everyone around was hushed, thinking we were the worst parents in the whole world, lowlifes who should never have been allowed to have kids.

Ann gulped and snuffled as the log began its slow ascent to the top of a mountain of boulders and then rocketed down into a pool of frothing water. We were doused with spray, wet and cold. Up, down, and around, up, down, and around. In a matter of minutes, the ride was over. Two hours of waiting in the most oppressive heat ever culminated in four minutes of soppy bliss.

Ann looked up at us, her cheeks glistening and her eyes glassy. "That was the funnest ever, ever, ever. Can we do it again? Can we? Please, please, plea…"

"No."

We wandered through the park, making stops at Goodtime Hollow and Fort Funtier, areas created for kids the size of ours. Except for being larger, they weren't any different from the playground at Twin Lakes Park in Paris, Illinois, sixteen miles from home. There was a carousel. Twin Lakes had a carousel. There were little cars. Twin Lakes had little cars. There were slides and swings. Twin Lakes had slides and swings. The biggest difference was that at Six Flags the rides were in direct sunlight and the plastic seats, like sizzling hotplates, blistered their little behinds. The rides at Paris were shaded by towering oak trees, and the plastic seats were cool as cucumbers.

At Pet-A-Pet, the girls scrambled from one farm animal to another. We live on a farm. We raise registered Polled Hereford cattle. Six

Flags had a couple of scrawny calves chewing on straw in a pen. We have a couple of bulls and dozens of cows and calves grazing on green fields. The girls have gone with their dad to feed motherless calves with bottles, and they've petted calves just hours after they were born. Neighbors have sheep and goats. Our cousins in Washington have a farm with pigs, chickens, bunnies, horses, goats, turkeys, donkeys, and an occasional nest of newborn mice. Essentially, we have our own petting zoo.

"When I'm eight and in 4-H, I want a white calf like the Six Flags calves," said Jaime.

"We raise Polled Herefords. They're red and white, not just white."

"But I want a white one, and, besides, ours aren't red, they're brown. Mr. Hodge the science teacher has a two-headed calf that died. It's brown and white. It's in the glass case by his classroom at school. He stuffed it. He got it in the winter. Somebody who lives in Metcalf called and said he should come get the two-headed calf that was just borned, but he had to teach his science class, so he told John the janitor to take the bus to pick up the dead calf that had two heads. But then a blizzard came, and John got stuck in a ditch, and then school was called off early, and there wasn't enough buses to get the kids home because John was stuck in the ditch with the died calf. I'm hungry."

We left Six Flags. A few miles down the Interstate at St. Charles, Missouri, massive against the hot white sky, was the second installment of our Escapade of Fun and Educational Entertainment—Noah's Ark Restaurant and Hotel. The restaurant was a replica of the ark, its enormous hull made of wood planks painted dark red. I'm not sure if it was cubit-by-cubit accurate, but it was a colossal ship, big enough to house hundreds of people in the dining areas, the special "cage" rooms, and the Raven's Rest cocktail lounge. A menagerie of giant fiberglass critters and their mates sprawled on the decks and poked their heads through the portholes.

A five-times-larger-than-life fiberglass Noah stood on the bow, one hand raised toward heaven. I couldn't tell if the bird on his arm, which looked more like a bloated seagull than a dove, had just come in for a skid landing or was readying for the big olive branch release. A fiberglass elephant reared up in front of the restaurant with its trunk curled around an American flag, and his mate peered out a cabin window. Two giraffes extended their heads out of the roof, looking toward the stern. Various big cats lazed on the roof. Anticipating rapturous expressions, JR and I turned to the girls, excited to see their faces. Their heads were cocked to the side.

"Why is there a ship in the parking lot?" one of the girls asked.

"How did a ship get from the Mississippi to here?" asked the other. "And why is that man with the bird on the top of the ship bigger than the elephant?"

"We'll explain it all when you're older," we said.

A waitress in a leopard-print miniskirt, wearing a safari helmet, whisked us by the brown plastic chairs shaped like bears, past the hippo robot, and to our table. I held my breath, hoping that Ann wouldn't see the hippo, its mechanized toothy mouth chomping on pennies. We didn't need another Chuck E. Cheese moment. She passed safely. We ordered and waited. And waited.

"What kind of lighting did Noah have on the ark?" asked JR, trying to keep the girls from beating on the table with their forks.

"Huh?"

"Flood lights!"

"What are flood lights?

"We'll explain it when you're older."

Finally, our drinks arrived. The girls were enamored completely with the orange plastic swizzle sticks shaped like giraffes. They churned their lemonades into mini-cyclones, swirling them counterclockwise and then clockwise, sending tsunamis into the cracker basket. They extricated the sticks from all four of the drinks and bounced them across the table like pogo sticks. The giraffes danced and kissed and somehow knocked over Ann's lemonade. Which sent her into a crying fit. Which meant we needed one more lemonade. Which came with one more swizzle stick. Five swizzle sticks and two girls. Do the math.

By the time the famous Noah's Ark clam chowder and the cheese burgers arrived, the girls had downed their drinks and had eaten two baskets of crackers. The table was littered with crumbs, their laps were littered with crumbs, the floor was littered with crumbs, and they were entertaining themselves by trying to transfer static-electrified cracker wrappers from one girl to the other. Neither was the least bit hungry.

The next morning we set off for the educational segment of The Escapade of Fun and Educational Entertainment—the St. Louis Zoo. By mid-morning, the temperature was already in the low 90s, and by afternoon, the temp was forecast to reach over 100, surpassing the all-time records for the 10th of August. Dedicated to my mission to educate, come hell or high water, I presented the girls with my first mini-lecture of the day. "Way back in the 1920s, the St. Louis Zoo got rid of cages and built natural environments with grottos, moats, fountains, and pools. It was one of the first zoos in the entire world to try to copy the animal's natural habitat. A grotto is ..."

"There's a tiger in a cage in the Madeline book," said Jaime.

"A really scary tiger with big sharp teeth," said Ann, her pink bifocals steaming up in the heat.

I motioned toward the bear bluffs, pointing out the rock caverns for snoozing, the fallen trees for back scratching, and the pools for swimming.

"I like our pool better. It doesn't have rocks in it, and we have a blue slide. You yell at us if we throw rocks in the pool."

"Let's take a look at the grizzlies," I said, heading over to read the information placard. "This is so interesting. Grizzlies can run faster than horses. Over 30 miles an hour. The scientific name for grizzlies is Ursus arctos horribilis. Horribilis. Now that's an interesting word. But bears aren't horrible, they ..."

"Where's the bears? I don't see any bears."

Apparently, the grizzlies were napping. Next stop, Andean bears.

"Andean bears have white circles around their eyes. Like they're wearing glasses."

"But where are they?"

"Maybe we can find some Malayan Sun bears. Sun bears nest in trees and their tongues are really long so that they can poke them into termite hills. They think termites are really, really yummy."

"Yuck. But where are they? I want to see sun bears."

Even the sun bears were avoiding the sun. Obviously, all of the bears were reclining in the cooler confines of their caves. As were the lions, tigers, leopards, zebras, antelopes, elephants, monkeys, llamas, and every other species of animal. It was just too darn hot.

"Mom, this is boring, just looking at caves and animals that look dead. Can we just go home and go swimming?"

We turned up the air conditioner in the station wagon and hit the highway. When we got back to the farm, Grandma and Grandpa asked the girls what was their favorite part of the trip.

"The playground at Burger King where we stopped on the way home!" they yelled simultaneously.

❦

THE FOLLOWING SUMMER WE told the kids that if they'd like to plan a short getaway before school started, we'd consider their proposal. They grabbed pencil and paper and held a summit meeting behind the closed doors of the girls' bedroom. It wasn't long before they returned to the family room.

"I'm president," said Jaime. "And secretary...because Ann and Marcus can't write."

"I'm vice president," said Ann. "Marcus isn't anything."

"Here's our list."

> Go to McDonald's in Paris and get Happy Meals
> Go to the late movie at the Paris Theater

Get popcorn and don't have to share
Come home and stay up as late as we want
Mom and Dad have to go to bed but we don't
The End

Advice to parents of young children: Let the kids plan the vacation.

Epilogue: In 2010, at the age of 63, I made my first trip to Disneyland. Ann took me. She planned the trip. She and her husband named their daughter Autumn Elizabeth Roll-Stanaway. Twenty-eight letters will definitely fill a nameplate on the corner office door.

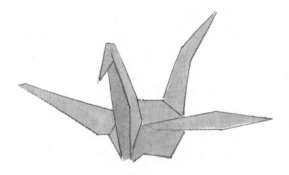

TWINS

WHEN MEGAN, OUR FIRST-BORN grandchild, was three, I asked her what she wanted to be when she grew up. "A daddy," she said.

"Why a daddy?"

"Because daddies get to leave their string cheese wrappers anyplace they want."

Meg has twin brothers, Jack and Andy. Wherever the family went, people stopped to fuss over the babies in their twin-except-for-color outfits. Jack always wore blue and Andy wore green. That way we could tell them apart. Andy has a tiny freckle on his forehead, but you have to be up close and personal to see it. People smile at single babies, but they "attack" twins. They have a million questions about twins. Our daughter Jaime and her husband Jim learned early on that if they wanted to get any shopping done, they needed to put one baby in a shopping cart, the other baby in another cart, and take off in different directions.

One evening they went out for pizza. The babies were in their twin carriers on the table. Person after person stopped to gush about the beautiful babies. Jaime was always careful to introduce their big sister Meg so that she wouldn't feel left out. That evening a dozen people put their faces into the carriers and cooed at the babies, and every time, Jaime introduced Meg. But then, person number 13 came up, and while trying to wipe slobber off the babies' faces, eat a slice of pizza, clean up Meg's spilled milk, Jaime forgot to mention Meg.

"But I'm cute, too," Megan said with tears in her eyes.

The question everyone has about twins is, "Are they identical?" By the time the babies were only a few months old, we had been asked the question a thousand times. When we answered that we didn't know, people were frustrated. They were never satisfied and often didn't believe us when we said that the only way to tell is with DNA. So we told Jaime we'd spring for the test. Besides, we were all curious, too. Well, with three little kids, a full-time job, and all the other hats a mom must wear, Jaime never got around to getting the cheek swabs. We sat her down and said that the boys' fifth birthday present was the DNA test. Get the kit.

The results came back and Jaime gathered the boys and Meg for the announcement.

"Boys, you're identical!"

"What's 'identical' mean?" asked Jack.

Jaime had not anticipated this question.

"Well, it means that there was one egg and it split ..."

"Does that mean we're chicks?" Andy shouted.

The boys are now in kindergarten. The other day they had to fill out a work sheet about their family. One question was "What does your grandma do?" Jack answered, "She's a teacher." Andy answered, "She cooks for me." Another question was "What does your grandpa do?" Andy answered, "He makes everything okay." Jaime asked him how grandpa made everything okay. Without hesitating, Andy cocked his head and responded as if the answer was obvious, "With a flashlight."

MISSING BODY PARTS

I'M A SUCKER FOR women's magazines. Get me to a doctor's appointment early, and I'll scramble through the waiting room, search for the newest editions, stack them up, and dig in. If the doctor is running late, no problem. I'll occupy myself with articles about anything from "I Married My Daughter's Boyfriend's Stepfather" to "21 Celebrities Discuss How to Do a Brazilian Bikini Wax at Home."

From my reading, I've determined that most women don't like their bodies. One magazine says that 88 percent of women dislike at least one part of their bodies. Jessica Alba is among the 88 percent. She says, "My breasts are saggy, I've got cellulite ... every actress out there is more beautiful than me." Obviously, Jess missed the two dozen surveys that say she is the Sexiest Woman in the World. (She also missed junior high-school English or else she would have said "more beautiful than I.") It's also obvious that the girl has never looked at herself in a full-length mirror while she's wearing the leather Dark Angel outfit. Jennifer Love Hewitt, a former *TV Guide*'s pick for "Sexiest

Woman on TV," bemoans that her "legs look like Popeye's drumsticks." Angelina Jolie, whose lips, according to plastic surgeons, are the most often wished-for lips of all time, hates her—you guessed it—lips.

I, too, am among the 88 percent. I worry over any number of body parts, but one body part in particular has bothered me the most. People who know me would say, "Breasts, hands down. Look what you've been through!" Think October. The Month of Pink. Wal-Mart thinks pink. Ford Motors thinks pink. Even "real" men think, and wear, pink. It's impossible not to think about breasts, boobs, tatas, and titties in October. We're inundated by slogans: "I pink I can, I pink I can"; "Boobs: They could use your support"; "Walkin' my buns off for boobs"; "Thanks for the mammaries." No getting around it, breasts are a big deal in the United States. And big breasts are a bigger deal. Ask any guy. You'd think that I, because I hardly have any, would obsess most about my breasts.

A decade and a half ago, chunks of breast #1, the one on the right, were rooted out, and the whole thing was detached in toto a few years later. After a suspicious-looking mammogram, breast #2 was whittled away to pancake size before the docs decided that everything was A-okay. By that time, I couldn't even fill a size AAA bra. With padding. I'm told by magazine articles that those of us who have concave chests are supposed to mourn the loss of those sensuous globes of womanhood. But, as far as I'm concerned, they're just stains on a couple of slides under a microscope. (Also, my breastlessness is part of my back-up plan if the state legislature decides to decrease my teacher's pension. I'll apply to Hooters, fail the physical, and sue for a truckload of cash on the grounds of discrimination against the breastless.)

In actuality, the body part that has had the greatest impact on my life and has created the most turmoil and unrest is my toenail. Precisely, the toenail of my big toe on my left foot. This toenail has caused me to awaken in the middle of the night in a cold-sweat panic. It has caused me to keep an emergency supply of Band-Aids in my Books Are Fun book bag and has even caused me to wear socks with Birkenstocks.

The ordeal began three years ago. After swabbing my toenail with remover to soak off the Diamond Strength No Chip polish that had lasted since Christmas, my eyes bugged out like ping-pong balls. No longer was the nail of my left big toe pink and curved like a seashell. It was yellowish, and it was detaching at the sides from the nail bed. What if my toenail was trying to turn thick? And yellow green? With fungus? What if it started to smell like a back alley dumpster? I dug under the nail with a tool from the manicure set my brother gave me for high school graduation. The nail lifted. It was as loose as a flake of shale. Soon I was poking a toothpick halfway down the nail. Then I tried the blade of a plastic knife. Just when I thought the entire nail would disengage and fly off like a satellite, the knife blade stuck. My nail was hanging to the bed by a scrap of crepe-y skin.

It was almost spring, and the high school prom was coming up. I had to go — teachers were expected to chaperone. You'd think that someone who qualified for free senior drinks at Burger King could not care less about prom. But the truth is I had new shoes that I was dying to show off. They were black and strappy, high heeled, open-toed sandals — it's hard to find sexy in size 10!

Every day I checked my toe, and every day, my discomfort ratcheted up a notch. Before long, I had developed a raging case of debilitating big toe panic. To complicate matters, I had age-old issues with dances. When I looked at my toe, something about the decomposing nail catapulted me back to decades of less-than-happy memories. I remembered the high school and college dances I wasn't invited to. I remembered how my husband listed dancing as a requirement for a good wife, but he said dancing with me was like dancing with a fence post.

Night after night, I appealed to the gods of all religions to save my toenail before prom. Surely the gods would get it. Barefoot Buddha measured the universe by walking seven steps in each of its corners.

Barefoot Vishnu needed only three steps to map out earth, the intermediate world, and heaven. Christ, definitely, was a bare footer. I summoned help from Greeks and Romans with wings on their feet and holes in their heels. My panic intensified when my copy of *The Penguin Dictionary of Symbols* inadvertently fell open to page 398. Foot. "The foot is a symbol of the strength of the soul. Any deformity of the foot betrays a weakness of the soul." That's it. My toenail was a deformity that symbolized the pathetic and feeble weakness of my soul.

With prom just weeks away, I needed to do something. Something fast. Obviously, a podiatrist should be able to find the solution to my problem. I made an appointment with Dr. Killough. He was wearing cowboy boots. Who in his right mind wears cowboy boots to treat other people's feet? I can see Birkenstocks or Dr. Scholl's or even Crocs. But not lizard-leather, pinching, pointy-toed, high-heeled cowboy boots.

"Dead," he said. "The nail is dead. I'll just cut it out and off, and you'll have a new nail in a year."

"Excuse me? Did you say a year?"

"No worries. No infection, no fungus. Just get some nail polish and paint the skin. Or get a fake nail at Wal-Mart. No big deal."

Killough cut the nail right down the middle and right down each side and threw the pieces in the trash. The skin under where the nail had been was rough and ridged, brownish. Under magnification, it would have looked like a terraced Japanese rice paddy.

First stop after leaving the office, of course, was the cosmetics aisle at Wal-Mart. As someone who heretofore had no idea that "artificial nails" even existed, I was struck dumb. There were as many choices of fake toenails as there were of sliced bread. The major brand was made by ill-named Kiss Products, Inc. The Express On variety was sold in boxes of "24 Toenails in 10 sizes - double on popular sizes." I had no idea there were "popular" toenail sizes. Express On's were like stickers with "easy on, easy off" glue already applied to the back of each French-tipped nail. The "Patented Easy to Apply Self Tab!" variety came with 96 pure white nails and its own tube of "Pink Nail Glue." I carefully read the instructions on every box, even those written in Spanish. Every box said the same thing: Press the artificial nail onto the natural nail and hold for five seconds. Obviously, this presented a problem. I had no "natural nail."

I loaded my shopping basket with one box of every variety. I could have gotten away with spending $3.98 for one box, but what if I got the wrong kind? I rounded the corner, headed into aisle 8, and there in front of me stood my friend Marsha. Her cart was loaded with bottles of merlot and gourmet dinners for her four rat terriers. She eyed my basket for a second, and I unloaded on her, barely holding back the tears.

"My toenail is rotting off and it's worse than having my breast cut off or my teeth fall out and I have sexy shoes and it's almost prom and ..."

Marsha is a nurse, a slim, trim, petite version of a fairy godmother nurse who is always in make-everyone-feel-good mode. She pursed her tiny hot pink lips into an "o" and then frowned a little.

"Ohhhhhh, but you're pretty, no one will notice. It will be okay."

Marsha thinks everyone is pretty. She could look into the pop-eyes of someone drooling black spit and say, "Ohhh, sweet thing, you're so pretty." Marsha, I wanted to yell, you have tiny perfect toes with tiny perfect toenails tucked inside your pure white jogging shoes. And besides that, you have tiny ankles and long hair, and you even have a tanning bed in your own bedroom. Not that I'd ever use one because they remind me too much of coffins and I'm scared of skin cancer, but you always look like the smiling, golden "after" photo in magazine ads.

Marsha gave me a half-hug. I was afraid she was about to say something like "Remember the words of Helen Keller. 'The best and most beautiful things in the world cannot be seen, nor touched, but are felt in the heart.'"

"That really sucks," she said.

At home, I laid out my supplies. Scissors to trim the fake nail to fit. A file for shaping. Polish. Remover if I messed up. And the plastic tray of artificial nails from the box of 24 stick-ons. It took only a second to realize that the woman who needed the largest nails in the tray would have to be about 6'5" and wear a size 14 shoe. Then I remembered: drag queens. Kudos to Kiss, Inc. for making equal opportunity toenails.

I found the right size, a #3, and stuck it to my toe. It was a little crooked, but, no matter, this was just a trial run. I painted Insta-Dri Smudge-Proof Nail Color with Tea Tree Oil on each of my nails. Satisfied, I went to sleep. Sometime during the night, I awoke with the familiar cold sweat and the sinking feeling that I was naked in the town square, and everyone was pointing at my toe, shouting, "Grrrross, grooooss!"

When I woke up in the morning, my first thought was to fling back the covers to see my foot. There was no nail on my left toe. I thrashed around, threw the blankets to the floor. Still no nail. Then I felt it. It was stuck to the left cheek of my behind.

Every night before going to bed, I put a magnifying glass over my toe to see if a tiny bit of nail was growing at the base. Nothing.

In the days before prom, I obsessed about all the what-if's I could possibly imagine. What if the nail popped off and I went into the restroom and one of the girls, or worse, a colleague, looked under the door to see if the stall was occupied and spotted my toe, looking like dead sunbaked toad skin? What if the toenail snapped off, bounced onto the dais, and was in the spotlight when the queen was crowned. What if…

Finally it was time for the prom. I polished the skin under where the fake toenail would be. I stuck on the nail and polished it pretty with two layers of Pure Ice Envy #965. I put on the sexy, strappy, high-heeled sandals.

After stepping out of our car at the parking lot where the dance was being held, I realized it was dark outside. I couldn't see my fingertips, let alone my toenails. It was so dark, in fact, that I had to bend over to make sure I didn't trip on the curb. It was dark inside the ballroom. Dances are dark. Kids like dark, the darker the better. I couldn't see my toes at all. And neither could anyone else. The only worry I would have if I lost the nail was if I needed to use the restroom where the lights were on. I could keep my legs crossed for three hours.

Killough was right. It took a full year for the nail to grow back. With several hundred artificial toenails taking up space in my bathroom, I began making mental notes of what to do with them. Fake toenails hot-glued around a mirror would be just about as cute as those mirrors bordered with seashells from Florida. Or maybe I could cut them into circles, spray paint them silver and sew them on a Christmas sweater. Or maybe I could just leave them scattered by the back storage closet of my classroom where three different times I've found piles of sawed-off dirty fingernails.

Unfortunately, a few months after the toenail on my left big toe grew back, I cut the nail on my right big toe way too close. An ingrown toenail. The corner dug into the soft tissue on the side of the nail. Inflammation. Indescribable pain. Dr. Killough cut away the nail and covered the toe with fluorescent orange tape.

"No worries. It will grow back in a year."

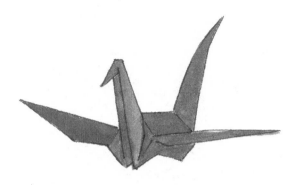

CANCER

IN MY GARDEN I CUT DEADHEADS — MARIGOLDS, ASTERS, DILL;
snip icicle pansies and basil; ask how did he cut me?

Hacking at my chest like frozen smut, or
slicing a tiny root.

How did he stitch? As I slip honeysuckle, looping,
over trellis and box?

Or like punching twine through shocks
tied to a post.

When he stapled, was it as I fit a frame,
or as wisteria embraces the arch.

In a public garden, Babylon,
he split me open and tapped my breast.

TO DR. URETZ OLIPHANT

WHEN WE SHAKE HANDS, my hand, in the pink palm of yours, is small … and white. Your hand is black with yellowish knuckles and dark creases, and huge. Your grip is firm and your hand is warm. Dry like a sun-warmed clay pot. Only one other black man has ever touched me. Eugenio … who wanted to be my boyfriend when I was twenty-two and lived in Brazil.

But you … you have been assigned to me. You tell me your name, and it is a jumble of syllables that I can't remember, a first name like the city in the Netherlands that begins with u. A last name that sounds like "elephant." Your job is to cut it off, my right breast. The breast that peeked, once, out of a crocheted halter top and teased my husband into submission, the breast that fed three babies until they could hold cups on their own. It filled out my dresses and took on all comers when I stood up tall and straight.

You promise to take good care of me. You tell me I'm in good hands.

❦

As soon as someone said the c-word, I wanted the thing off, but that's never the way it goes. There's the "wait time," the "character-building time," as my mom would say. Wait…and think…and feel. Then mourn. So, I read seed catalogs and dream of fiddling in the garden, a way to occupy the hours, minutes, and seconds until your hands will do their work. I think of cutting dried marigolds, dead and dying, from their stems, and snipping the yellow dust crowns of dill because, without blooms, the feathery greens for mincing over new potatoes and poached fish will grow thicker. Pansies will be pinched and set in small vases on the kitchen counter. So will the flower-flecked stalks of sweet basil. Deadheading empowers the plants to produce more leaves, more blossoms, and seeds.

When I think of cutting and pruning, I wonder how you will cut me. I think about the salmon cannery, down the beach from my house, where I worked one summer during college. With your huge hands, will you hack away at me as I, back then—in automatic, distracted by books and by boys—sawed the flesh of fish?

Or will you slice and sliver me as if I were a dove?

When I remember slipping honeysuckle and clematis vines in and out of the trellis, looping the tendrils through lattice crosses, I wonder how you will sew me. I always handle blossoms as if they're spun glass, positioning them face-up toward the sky. Even the breeze of my moving hand is enough to loosen the blossoms from their curling vines. How will you handle me? Will you be as gentle? Will you stitch me, in and out, over and under, the tiny needle in your huge hands held tight between your fingers, with as much care as when I lift vines to the sun?

Or will you jab the needle in as if you were punching twine into a cold turkey, yanking the string to a hard knot?

Maybe it won't be stitches at all. Maybe you'll use staples, crisscross tracks like bird prints in the snow. I think about my students' poems and stories, their admission essays, their words on pages, and how I staple them just so, and how we have a laying on of hands before I slide them into envelopes and send them out into the world to be judged. Maybe you'll wince with each push and breathe with the release. Maybe you will...and maybe you won't.

What will you think about? Your own wife? Your daughter...do you even have one? Last night's ball game? Changing the oil in your car? You're a man. How can you know what I am feeling? What will I be when you complete your work?

※

WHEN IT IS DONE, after you have finished the job, I have no answers for my questions. There are no memories, only an aching tenderness in my chest even bigger than your hand. Stemmed through with tubes that look like vines and with seepings of blood like Rorschach roses, I'm sick, swimming up through oceans of tangled anemones that circle and wave in currents of nausea. I'm seeing double and doubled over with morphine. But there are flowers in the room, and their colors and their scents are lifting me toward light.

※

IN THE HOURS AFTER surgery, I get to know you better. You are a gentle man. I think you must have cupped the rose of my breast in your hand, slipped it gently into the glass marked "Urgent," a word that sounds something like your name, and carried it down the fluorescent-bright hallway to the lab. You would have waited for the report, waited to hear that you got it all, and returned to assure me.

At my bedside, with your hand on mine, you tell me that the Amazons cut off their right breasts to better shoulder their bows for the hunt. You don't even know that once, a long time ago, I lived in Brazil.

I tell you that even though it's winter now, come spring I will arm myself with a trowel, a hoe, and a pail of water. I will set in seeds, and they will grow. And I will grow. I promise.

You lift your hand from mine and nod. Yes, you say, yes.

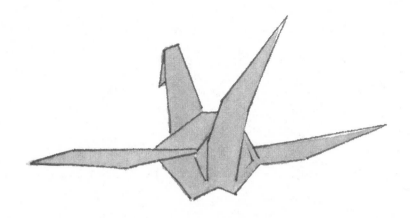

A Thousand Cranes

I wish I could take off my own boots, but someone else does the twisting and pulling, grunting and groaning for me. Like I'm Cinderella's stepsister. When I dropped a jelly bean the other day, I wanted to dive for it, but someone else hit the floor, snatched it up, and popped it into my hand before the five-second rule ran out. Someone drives me where I need to go, someone carries my groceries, and someone does my laundry. (Ninety percent of the time, the "someone" is JR, my husband, the man I've lived with in the same house for 37 years, and who, until recently, never knew where the pot holders were kept.) You could say I live like a queen, like Cinderella herself just before the happily-ever-after end of the story. When I tell people that I live like a queen, their usual comment is, "Wow! Lucky you, I'd love to have someone do everything for me!"

The truth is, being a queen sucks.

My status was elevated to queen back in January when my doctors found that cancer was chewing up the bones in my back. I am not allowed to bend or to lift anything over ten pounds or to push or to pull. It's ironic that when I envision the cancer, I see it as an army of mini Jaws of Life gnashing their way down my spine with shark teeth pincers and bone crunching claws. Jaws of Life. I guess I should try my darnedest to reverse the image, make my meds and infusions into the Jaws of Life and the cancer thing-ys into blind, newborn mole rats not long for this world.

Most of the time, I'm able to push all the crappy stuff to the back of my mind and keep a smile on my face, but today I had a Reality Check, capital R, capital C.

On my way to meet with several doctors in several different clinics in two different towns, I stopped by the DMV.

"Well, what can I do for you? the clerk asked.

I opened my jacket and pointed to my back. I introduced her to what I call "my big, black OLD-age ninja turtle" brace. It's a contraption of corseted cords in the back; Velcro fasteners front, back, and sides; plastic and metal. It goes over my shoulders and cinches tight at my waist. The manufacturer dolled it up by embroidering purple and silver stars a la Star Wars on the front and white laces up the back like something out of Gone with the Wind. The brace keeps me upright and straight as a soldier. My grandkids think I look like a super hero.

"Do you think I might qualify for disability parking?" I asked.

Her face softened into the soulful gaze I've gotten used to — the "oh-I'm-so-sorry" look. She nodded and fumbled through a drawer until she came up with a Persons with Disabilities Certification for Parking Placard form. She kept her eyes down.

"Give this to your doctor and bring it back," she said quietly.

"Attitude is 90% of the battle," she added, looking up and into my eyes.

Any guesses as to how often I've heard the "attitude" remark? I know it's awkward for people. Hardly anyone knows what to say to someone with stage IV cancer. Like most people, I believe attitude is a major player in recovery or, in my case, survival for as long as possible. And, believe me, I'm definitely game for an all-out assault on the statistics. (Most of the time, I get an A+ for attitude.) But it's a lot of pressure to think my attitude is responsible for controlling my disease.

The latest issue of Living with Cancer took away a bit of the burden. The essay begins, "MYTH #1. A positive attitude is required to beat cancer." MYTH, in capital letters. The author wrote "...it's perfectly normal for you to experience a range of negative emotions, including sadness, grief, frustration and anxiety..." What a relief. Maybe those of us who are attitude-weary can relax a little. I'm pretty sure I've felt every single possible emotion there is, negative and positive, during this dance with cancer, and while sadness and grief creep in only occasionally, hardly at all, sometimes they take me to a very lonely dark corner.

I left the DMV and headed for the first appointment of the day. When I gave the form to the doctor, I was doing okay, at least an A- in attitude. I was thinking about how convenient the parking pass would be during rain storms and when the only spots open at the cancer center were on the open-air fourth level far away from the elevators. He gave me the "I'm-so sorry-look" and put his hand lightly on my knee.

I watched him fill in the answers and make checks here and there. As I said, I was doing okay. But when he ignored "Disability is temporary" and made a big "X" on the line next to "Disability is permanent," I could feel the tears coming. I was caught completely off guard. It was the same unexpected reaction I had when, 37 years ago, JR said, "We're eating Whitey." We had just moved to the farm, and I had gotten to know the cattle. I scratched them behind the ears, and I even named some of them. Having never lived on a farm before, I hadn't made the connection that some of them would be slaughtered and would end up on the dinner table. The words "eating Whitey" opened the floodgates, and I sobbed uncontrollably.

When I saw "Permanent disability," I didn't sob, but I was overwhelmed with sadness and grief. It was a reality check that I had, so far, failed to fully acknowledge and accept. I snuffed back the tears, chin up, shoulders straight, and left the clinic.

It was a long day. I thumbed through magazines and watched a video on my cell phone of my granddaughter laughing to get me to the next appointment. I smiled through the same procedures over and over. Temperature. Blood pressure. Same questions at every appointment. Pain level from 0 to 10 with zero being no pain and 10 being severe pain. Fatigue level, 0 to 10.

I came home after dark. Exhausted. A day that had started with a fatigue level of 2 ended with a full-fledged fatigue level of 10. And I was sad. I felt the grief of knowing I might never get better, that the goal of my doctors was to manage my pain and to try to keep the cancer from spreading, but that there was no cure.

As I was taking off my jacket, I noticed that on my desk was a large box wrapped in brown paper. It was from Denver, from JR's cousin Rick, his Japanese wife Mingmei, and their children, Alex and Hannah.

I slit through the packing tape with a knife, spread open the lids, and, at first glance, through the blur of bubble wrap, saw a rainbow of color…pink, orange, chartreuse, red, green, blue, violet, yellow. At second glance, I realized that what I was seeing, tucked carefully inside the box between the packing and crumpled newspapers, were strings and strings of tiny origami cranes. I knew the significance of the cranes immediately, and I knew that if I were to count them, there would be a thousand.

Seven years ago, the students and staff at the high school where I taught folded and strung together a thousand paper cranes for a former student who was undergoing her second stem cell transplant. The legend is that if family and friends fold a thousand paper cranes, a loved one will recover from illness and live a long life. One thousand wishes. One thousand symbols of hope.

Finally, at the end of the day, I allowed the tears to come again, this time in overwhelming recognition of the words, "There is no greater gift than hope."

II

BRASIL WITH AN S:
A MEMOIR

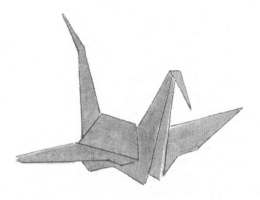

DAD

THIS WOULD BE MY first trip alone. I tried to tell myself I
was ready. I had a college degree. I had a teaching job at
the American School with a salary over $5000. Twenty-one,
legal, on my own, I was supposed to be composed and capable, even
a little worldly after spending seven months studying in London
and hitchhiking around the continent with my travel buddy Diane.
But I'd never traveled all by myself.

Hugs from my mom, my sister, and my brother. Then the unexpected. My dad—never one to be demonstrative, except with our wie-
ner dog and his Springer spaniels—teared up, hugged me hard, and
told me he loved me. He had never said those words to me before,
and I wouldn't hear them again until 1991 when I made the 2500-
mile road trip in the dead of winter to say goodbye to him before
he died. For my whole life, he had been distant. Today, of all days,
he made me cry. I sobbed onto the plane. My seatmate, someone's
grandfather I was sure, offered me his handkerchief, a travel pack
of tissues, and, finally, to make me laugh, the barf bag.

Dad. I was like him. I looked like him. And I could get just as angry about injustice as he did, but, unlike him, I rarely opened my mouth. I kept my anger stewing inside me. He had graduated from the University of Washington—the school all three of us kids, a generation later, would attend—and had immediately, but not necessarily by choice, gone off to Italy to save the world from the Nazi terror. He left the Northwest as a happy-go-lucky recent college grad, but with one foot still metaphorically firm on the farm. He came home from the war scarred, the strong, silent type, smoking three packs of cigarettes a day.

When we were little, we would push back his sleeves and touch the wrinkled whorls of skin, the size of quarters and half-dollars. To us, the scars meant hero. Pulling down the tin box on the top shelf of his closet, fingering the bars of ribbon and shiny medals, we begged for stories of roaring fighter jets, zinging bullets, and the enemy staggering, flailing and falling backwards into mud. But he just said, "War is hell. That's all I've got to say."

An accountant, Dad showed up at dinner every night at 5:30, read every word—even the classifieds—of two newspapers, one from Anacortes—my hometown, the gateway to the San Juan Islands in Northwest Washington—and one from big-city Seattle.

He could do things we couldn't. From a thousand yards, he could spot a lady slipper orchid curling out of pine needles or a quail egg nesting in a spongy meadow. He knew history, geography, and politics. Politics he knew viscerally, in every cell of his body—so much so that after his first heart attack, when he was only 45, the doctor wrote on his chart that he was forbidden to read a paper or watch the news. Mere mention of Richard Nixon sent him into a rage.

Our favorite pastime with him was to spin the globe, point to a place—the more syllables, the better—and challenge him to tell us where it was. Tegucigalpa. Sea of Okhotsk. Bangkok. Rio de Janeiro. He never missed.

Years ago, he had left for parts unknown. Now it was my turn.

SUSAN

MY FIRST STOP ON the way to Rio was San Francisco, to visit my beautiful college roommate. Susan's long, thick hair was the color of honey. Ever since I'd met her three years before, I'd wondered what it would have been like if she'd been a red-head or a brunette, because her middle name was not the usual Ann or Marie; it was Honey, like her hair.

For several days, at her side, I explored the city, walking the wharves, pitching quarters at mimes and sleepy-eyed sax men, wandering through art galleries in Sausalito, and hanging on cable cars. Feeling smug that not so long ago, Diane and I had seen Europe on a couple of dollars a day, I watched as Susan peeled off twenties and fifties and left ten-dollar tips for muffins and coffee. Hers was a life of privilege. But I always remembered what my mom had said about her. "She's rich, but she's the most generous, kind, caring person you've ever brought home. She made us feel at home in our own house!" Those were comments I hoped someone someday would say about me. I knew the "rich" part would be a stretch, but maybe the rest was possible.

Susan pushed me into shops, their doorways hung with tinkling bells and bamboo chimes, where herbal smells and spices bit my nose and made me sneeze. Exotic to me meant my mom's stewed chicken with curried rice and fresh pineapple. But at restaurants with fresh flowers and napkins starched into swans, Susan ordered dinner in French, learned from a nanny when she was little. She taught me to eat hearts of palm and white asparagus wrapped and tied with slivered strips of pimento. She took me to a Middle Eastern café where we ate with our fingers in a curtained cubicle. At the top of the fanciest hotels, waiters called her "Miss Susan" and led us to the tables with the best view of Union Square and the Golden Gate Bridge. We were served sunset-colored cocktails, iced over in frost and blooming with ikebana. Each night we tumbled into our beds, and I replayed the day, smiling, but feeling a lot like a foreigner in my own country.

"Quit spending money on me," I said to her, feeling awkward.

"But I want to. It makes me feel good, and I need to feel good right now. Let me. Please," she said.

We left town and headed to her family's lodge in the mountains. We ran the trails with Oliver, her terrier, and one afternoon, she said, "You know, it's easier to talk to Ollie than it is to people." I nodded, but I couldn't find the right words to say to her. We sunned at the lake. She lent me a bikini, and I was embarrassed by so much white skin.

On the last day, she tucked gifts in my suitcase — a bag, red woven, with roosters on it from Portugal, bought in Lisbon; a coin purse from Spain, bought in Madrid; the brass egg, our symbol of new beginnings, that we had passed back and forth during college. As I was packing, she cried. For a few days, with me, she had been taken out of life as she knew it that summer. Peter, her brother — I saw photo after photo of him — in one, he was suspended horizontally along the jib sheet of a sailboat; in another, he was skiing a double diamond black run down a mountain slope in the Rockies — was dying of a brain tumor. Wherever we went, whatever we did, I knew she was thinking of him, curling up guilty inside herself because he'd turned angry, and she didn't know him, or herself, anymore.

"Make each day count," she said. "You just never know…"

First Impressions

MY FRIEND THEREZA MET me at the airport. Outside, everything was green, a thousand different greens—bluish, pinkish, and purplish green. Blinding yellow green. Swatches of brilliance were made brighter by sun after the early morning rain. Never had I seen such straight-up-to-the-sky mountains, rising up over vertical jungles of curling vines and flapping loose-leaved trees.

As we drove through town to Thereza's house, I was amazed by the luxurious buildings. Uniformed doormen stood out front, protected from the rain by awnings, and gardeners in raincoats pinched dying blossoms from overfilled planters. Men swept the black and white mosaic walkways and picked cigarette butts out of sand-filled garbage can-size ash bins. I noticed verandas with covered patio furniture, closed-up umbrellas, and potted leafy palms. Walls of windows looked out to the ocean. I also noticed again the steep mountains rising right out of the ground. But on these mountains, clinging to the sides, were hundreds and hundreds of ramshackle shanties.

❧

FIRST DAY AT MY own apartment. It was nothing like the small cramped rooms I'd lived in during my college years. A large living room and dining area. A tiny kitchen, but functional. Gas range, refrigerator, double sink. Three spacious bedrooms with hardwood floors and banks of windows. I twirled like a little kid over the gleaming floors in the master bedroom. It was twice as big as the other rooms. Two beds. Two dressers. A wall of closets. A full-length mirror. I had always shared; I'd never had my own room.

Connected to the bedroom was my own bathroom. Besides the usual sink and toilet, it had a bidet, just like those in fancy Paris hotels, and a walk-in shower separate from the tub. The floor was a mosaic of tiny black and white squares and diamonds, and the walls were made of sheets of gray speckled marble.

I went back into the bedroom and flopped onto one of the two beds. Through the windows, standing at the top of the 2330-foot mountain Corcovado, the Hunchback, was the statue of Christ the Redeemer, his arms stretched out to the world, his benevolent eyes looking down on all of Rio, rich and poor alike. I'd seen Corcovado on dozens of post cards and on every tourist brochure, but here he was, magnificent, right outside my window.

Like a white rocket, the statue rose skyward, into a heavy golden mist that billowed up, encircled his head, spilled to his feet, poured down the mountainside, and fell over the jungle-forest like water. This was the sight I would wake up to every morning, every day. I went to the window, opened it, and looked down. There I saw a shivering tree of avocados. Besides strawberries, avocados were one of my all-time favorite foods. Behind the tree, a man and woman embraced, unaware that I was watching them.

Back in the kitchen, four tiny pinkish chameleons clustered where the walls met the ceiling. Over time, I would not only get used to chameleons, but I would appreciate them—they gobbled up insects by the dozens. I would watch the pulsing of their blue-veined bodies as I worked in the kitchen. They would shift their heads and follow me with their eyes. I got so I could catch them and let them curl around my wrist and fingers. My kitchen buddies.

In Washington, there were no bugs. No one used screens on windows. In Brazil, there were bugs bigger than my hand. Waking in the middle of the night, needing a drink, I would have to make a decision. Should I turn on the light, or should I tiptoe across the floor in the dark? If I turned on the light, I would see hundreds of zigzagging cockroaches skedaddle across the linoleum or skitter over the counter, slip down the cupboards, and scramble under the oven. If I left the light off, I would step on them. Under slippered feet, they crunched.

Every couple of months, the exterminators came. They sprayed colorless, odorless DDT in every nook and cranny. Years later, when I was diagnosed twice with breast cancer, I wondered if Brazilian DDT could have been the cause. After the surgeon chopped off my right breast, I let out a sigh and followed it with a silent war whoop, acknowledging the renewal of my kinship with Brazil, bonded as a sister to those Amazon women who replaced their breasts with bows and arrows.

❧

MY ROOMMATE KAREN WAS a redhead with milk-white skin. She wore huge black and white checkerboard sunglasses. Later I would learn that her eyelashes were white, but every few months, her beautician back home in Dallas dyed her brows and lashes dark. She would sit motionless in a chair for forty-five minutes with her eyes pinched shut, knowing that if the dye touched her eyeball, she could go blind. After a few days, she made me her mission. Women from Texas knew how to fix a face, and mine needed some work. Before I knew what hit me, she had plucked and shaped my ragged brows into two swooping bird wings.

My other roommate, Ellen, was six feet tall with sun-streaked brown hair to her waist. She was muscled like a Michelangelo sculpture. In reality, she sometimes stood in for the supermodel Veruschka at long photo shoots. When passersby in Manhattan, thinking she was Veruschka, asked for her autograph, Ellen just scribbled a signature on a napkin or signed a coaster. It was easier than explaining.

Raised in Panama—her father piloted ships through the canal—she had traveled from continent to continent, picking up famous friends as others collected stamps or coins. She had left a seven-foot boa constrictor at home in Connecticut in the care of her mother. To celebrate turning 28, she had spent the past week shooting the rapids in Colorado, and she had the bruises, bug bites, and Band-Aids to prove it.

On our second day together, the three of us decided to walk from our apartment to the beach, three blocks away. Having come from the summer-chilly Northwest, I considered anything in the 70s hot, and I needed to get to water. The beach was nearly empty. Occasionally someone jogged by, and we could see a fisherman or two casting lines from an outcropping of rocks to the north.

We skipped along the shore, our feet bare, dashing in and out of the waves, squealing. Then a candle, half burnt, washed up against Karen's foot.

"Hey, look at this," she yelled.

Then another candle rolled up, and then another. Soon dozens of candles were swirling at our feet. All were white, all partly burnt. We noticed that candles littered the beach as far as we could see, some ebbing with the waves, others scattered slipshod in the sands up shore.

"Grab some up," Ellen said. "They're perfect for getting a little ambience into the ol' residência."

I was skeptical, but we had already established roles—Ellen was the leader, I was the follower, and Karen tried to keep a balance between the two of us. We chose the longest and the driest candles, stacking them neatly in our arms. As we were picking them up, we noticed more treasure. Coins, and even paper bills, half buried in the sand. A comb. Bottles of wine. Flowers, wet and wilting.

Our arms filled with candles and our pockets filled with money, we returned to the apartment, excited but a little suspicious. The next day I told Thereza. She turned green. "Oh, my gosh! Quick," she whispered, adding a litany of Portuguese phrases to her English. "Gather them up. We've got to get them back to the beach. Now…before it's too late. Maybe it's already too late.

"These candles are macumba," she explained. "Voodoo. Used in a ceremony to make some god happy. The coins, to bribe some god for protection. Or for luck. Thank goodness, they're white, not black. If they were black, they would have been for a curse. No one in Brazil — no one at all, it doesn't matter what your beliefs are, no one messes with macumba."

"During the seventeenth century," Thereza said, "millions of Africans were brought to Brazil to work in the sugarcane fields. Some say four or five million; others say closer to thirteen million. They came mostly from the Yoruba nation of West Africa, and they brought their gods with them. The Portuguese Jesuits, of course, forbid the worshipping of these gods, so the slaves got around the ban by renaming them as Catholic saints. Ogum, the god of war, became St. George; Iansa, the goddess of the winds and storms, St. Barbara; Omolu, the god of healing, St. Lazarus."

We learned to regard macumba rituals with respect. We checked our doorknobs for hairs tied in loops, a sure sign of a curse. We bypassed crossroads where white candles encircling elaborate displays of perfume, mirrors, lace, and crystal-clear bottles of cachaça — sugar cane rum — had been set out to entice a goddess. We sidestepped shrines of black candles, charred wood, cigars, black bottles of cachaça and black feathers on jungle trails just a few minutes walk from our apartment. We even learned to look down, hushed, when we walked by roadside stands cluttered with garish paintings of gods, strands of beads dangling with symbols of good fortune or bad luck, and fetishes for every wish, every ailment, every curse.

Our friend Dick, who had taught at the EA (Escola Americana do

Rio de Janiero, the American School) for several years and was now the guidance counselor, once dated a girl who had grown up macumba. After they broke up, for months, he spent every Friday, Saturday, and Sunday sick in bed. He swore he'd been cursed.

Dick lived in the building next to us. He was our resident "pharmacist." We depended on him to give us the right stuff to get us out of bed when we were laid up with the trots or stomach bugs. He had lived in Brazil long enough to know every worm and parasite that might adopt our blood, bones, and organs. By our symptoms, he would prescribe the right concoction — most often, for me, the dark red liquid in the small brown bottle that smelled like metal. Prescriptions signed by doctors weren't necessary. Anyone could go to the pharmacy and order whatever was needed.

Soon two new male teachers, both named Peter, arrived. Peter Cooper, a Princeton grad who left Wall Street for a breather in Rio, came to teach history. He was a Baseball-Hall-of-Fame-Cooperstown-New-York Cooper, but he was basketball tall and lanky, not baseball stocky. We immediately made him our big brother and kept him on call for whenever we needed a male escort. Peter's "breather" turned into a lifelong attachment to American schools; he served in Paris, Tokyo, Bogotá, and is now back in Rio as the current EA headmaster.

The other Peter, Peter Lownds, described by the female Brazilian teachers as "murine for the eyes," came down to Rio via Yale Drama School and the Peace Corps. All of us were disappointed to find that he brought a pretty new wife with him. Peter's mother was Amy Lownds, who had been married to Bob Dylan. Each time Karen put her Bob Dylan tape in the player, and we sang along to "Lay, Lady, Lay," we fantasized that Dylan might just pop down to Rio to check on his ex-stepson, but he never came.

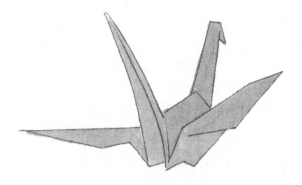

STRAWBERRIES

I N THE OUTDOOR MARKET, I gawked at papayas the size of footballs, persimmons the size of softballs, and bananas as long as ball bats. Thereza waggled her finger at me, insisting that everything that went into my mouth be thoroughly cleaned.

She kept an arsenal of purification concoctions — both fluids and pills — in small plastic bags and wide-mouthed jars. Bottled water only. Nothing fresh. I wanted passion fruit; she gave me rice. I wanted skewers of meat from street vendors; she gave me boiled-to-mush beans.

Day by day and bite by bite, I moved from canned American-type food to stewed what-have-you to an occasional morsel on my tongue of something fresh. Judith, Thereza's maid, was a marvelous cook. The kitchen smelled of herbs. Red-orange and golden sauces bubbled on the gas range. Lunch, course after course, was on the table at two, and dinner, again with course after course, was at eight. Each meal was followed by black coffee, thick with sugar, presented in dainty demitasse cups on a silver tray.

115

After a week or so of careful cuisine with no ill effects, Thereza gave me the okay to eat my first meal away from home. The entire family — parents, siblings, fiancés, grandparents, aunts, uncles, cousins — convened at a table in a neighborhood restaurant. Heaping baskets of bread. Plates of antipasto. Platters of chateaubriand and barbecued pork. Shallow dishes of vegetables submerged in sauces. Finally, for dessert, the waiter placed a bowl of gorgeous strawberries on the table — large, luscious, and red-ripe. I restrained myself for several minutes. But then I couldn't help myself. I zeroed in on one perfect specimen — red, almost glowing, with a perfect green crown. I needed that berry. "C'mon, Thereza, it'll be all right, I've eaten stuff for a whole week, não problema. Nada. Just one berry," I begged. I knew she wanted to slap my fingers, but finally she said, "Okay. One."

I plucked up the berry and popped it into my mouth. Sweet, juicy, luscious. Like no berry I had ever eaten before. One berry became two, and two became several. Before I knew it, I'd eaten a half dozen.

A few minutes later, they started — hives as big as quarters. Weals popped out on my cheeks, blossomed around my lips, and, in no time, covered me from head to foot. I was an itchy mass of urticaria-caused frenzy. Over the next three days, the raised patches speckled and disappeared from one part of my body, only to reappear again somewhere else — on my knees, over my forearms, on my chest. One eye was swollen shut. One cheek sagged like blubber. People came by the apartment to meet me, and I had to try hard not to cry. I could tell by their expressions that I horrified them — I was the hunchback of Notre Dame, the Elephant Man, the bearded lady at the sideshow.

Finally, I gave up. Convinced that I'd look like a monster for the rest of my life, I put on a large-brimmed hat, borrowed some sunglasses, and went outside for a little fresh air. Just as I rounded a corner, a street beggar hobbled up to me, her old face wizened up like a fig. She stretched her bony hands out to me. Then I looked at her, straight in the face. She had no eye. I decided there was a lesson I was supposed to learn.

Appropriately, this was the week of the moonwalk. I looked like an alien, and I felt like an alien. I was stumbling around in a Benadryl-induced stupor, drifting in and out of the foreign reality of my state of mind and of my new home. Lua, the Portuguese word for moon, was everywhere. On billboards, in the headlines, on TV. Even new Carnaval and bossa nova songs were moon-themed. Styrofoam spheres and tin foil space suits hung in shop windows, and space dioramas decorated counters and shelves. Everywhere, world-wide, people were talking about commander Neil Armstrong, command module pilot Michael Collins, and lunar module pilot Buzz Aldrin.

On the 16th of July, Thereza, Sonia, and I sat in front of the TV and watched them lift off, listening as Collins said, "...we are climbing like a dingbat," trying to imagine what it would be like to hurtle through space. Command module Columbia separated from the Saturn third stage, eased around, and connected its nose with the top of lunar module Eagle. Pieces of spacecraft drifted off and away. In awe, the three of us held our breath. (Years later, I would hold my breath again, knowing that components of a new shuttle were designed by my own brother.)

On the 20th, ten of us crowded again around the TV. When the commentary was in English, the nine Brazilians jabbered, but as soon as the commentary switched to Portuguese, they were silent, intent on every word. I strained my ears to hear recognizable words, begged for translations, and flipped through my dictionary. I looked at the bouncing grainy picture on the screen and tried my best to determine what was happening. When the astronauts landed in the Sea of Tranquility, we were anything but tranquil. That men were actually on the moon was both unsettling and mystifying. They said they went in peace for all mankind.

Amen, I thought.

ON THE ROCKS

KAREN TURNED THE KEY—we heard the click and the release of the first deadbolt, then the second. Earlier we had stopped by school to tie up a few loose ends, and, on the way home, we had picked up a couple of filets at a nearby meat market. With a salad, we'd have a simple, easy-to-fix dinner. I followed Karen into our apartment.

In the middle of the red couch, facing us straight on was Ellen, her long limbs extended, arms out—surely, a pose—legs spread wide open. Ellen as a six-foot x. Flexing her bare toes, she was waiting for us. And she had "the look"—the I've-got-something-up-my-sleeve-and-you'll-never-ever-in-a-million-years-guess-what-it-is look.

"Hold it. I think I need a beer," Karen said.

"No, ma'am, Miss Red-headed Naysayer. You are in for the most fantabulous treat of your life. Little lady, I am your ever-lovin' fairy godmother. Trust me."

Sighing, we shook our heads. Resigned. Still, we knew better than to miss an adventure with Ellen.

❧

We passed through familiar streets of apartment houses with first floor shops and small outdoor cafes, crossed several wide boulevards, went by the Hippie Fair in Ipanema, and after winding around jungle-covered mountains, finally emerged somewhere in Copacabana in a neighborhood of Easter-egg pastel-colored mansions, barely visible behind their swirly iron gates and walled gardens.

From Copacabana, our driver steered the car toward a dark mountain. At its base was the framework of a skyscraper, a bedlam of steel beams, ties, and girders. He pulled the car into a dirt lot and parked close to stopped-in-their-tracks backhoes, bulldozers, and dump trucks. Like a giant erector set or a Ferris wheel pulled straight, the structure rose heavenward, just shy of reaching the height of the mountain behind it.

By now, the sky was streaking flamingo pink, striped orange and purple. Against the sunset, the mountain looked blackish blue. The latticed towers of two monstrous cranes cast bent shadows, crisscrossing horizontally and vertically, reminding me of the black lines of Escheresque optical illusions. A few hundred yards from us was the multistoried framework of a superstructure, unfinished, floor over floor of layered concrete, wall-less and rust-tinged gray. Steel i-beams and girders reached straight up, out, and over from the immense foundation, a massive slab cluttered with saw horses, cinder blocks, and small wind-wisped dunes of powdery cement.

"Ellen? What in the ..."

"Shhhhh. Just follow me."

This was crazy. We were dressed up — just as Ellen had ordered us — but this was no party place; it was a verifiable hellhole. Ahead of us, she barged toward the building, plowing over ground soft from an early afternoon shower, striding over deep ruts, finally stepping onto a plywood catwalk that led to the first floor of the building.

Dumbfounded but trusting, as always, we followed her. She led us through stacks of dusty lumber to the center of the structure, stopping in front of a boxy freight elevator. By now, Karen's forehead had scrunched into a corrugation of wrinkles, and her lips were pursed tight. I was chewing the polish off my thumbnail. What if we were arrested? I'd heard stories of foreigners being locked up for decades, having to eat rats and mice raw, the American consulate just wringing his hands and sighing.

"Get on," Ellen said. "It's safe," she added, reading my mind.

"And you know that…how? This is a freight elevator, not exactly Marshall Fields," I said.

"Been here before … twice," she answered.

She wasn't going to give us even an inkling of what was what. Looking through the top of the wire mesh cage, I could see all the way up to the top of the building. Abandoned, obviously. Story after messy story of massive concrete platforms, piled one over the other. Ellen pushed a button, and the elevator creaked, jolted, and rocked upward. I was scared. Ellen was a risk taker; I was not. Although everyone thought I was a free spirit—after all, I had flown down to Rio on a one-way ticket—I was a coward, the type who'd put a toe into the water, draw back, and sit, arms locked, chin-to-knees safe on the shore of caution. My how-to-live-life manual was a list of musts, shoulds, coulds, nos, nevers, and nots; nowhere was there permission to enter a half-built skyscraper and joyride to the top.

Below me, through a hole in the floorboards, I could see the ground diminishing, as if I were looking down the shaft of a peashooter. Gulping heart throbs, I swallowed hard, sucking damp air down a throat drained dry. Soon the rusting yellow earthmovers were no more than sandbox toys, and the occasional taxi no bigger than a matchbox car. Gears grinding, slowly up we went. For an instant, lifting my eyes seaward, I caught a split second of blazing light, a narrow line of red orange squeezed between the darkening ocean and evening dusk. Then, once again, I was shot through with panic.

121

"Ellen, what are you doing? What are we doing? This has got to be illegal as hell."

"Never fear. It's okay. Trust me."

I'd heard those words before.

A single industrial-sized light bulb, attached to a thick cord and looped around a metal bar at the top of the elevator, provided the only light, sickish green and vapid. I could see the mountainside, dimly, cast black in the shadows. Spilled rocks, rubble, and riprap were trapped under an overlay of interlocking chain link, and I noticed that some-one had used heavy-duty wire cutters to snip holes in the protective barrier, a diamond pattern.

Finally the elevator jerked to a stop. We had arrived at the top floor, dead center of a giant steel door on a dark wall.

"Close your eyes. Close 'em tight. As soon as you hear the door open, take two steps forward," Ellen commanded.

The door whirred open, Ellen unlatched the elevator exit gate, and Karen grabbed for my hand. Eyes shut tight, together we stepped out, one step, two steps.

"Okay, open your eyes!"

Before us was not the confusion of trusses, struts, and beams as on the preceding floors. Before us instead was a dazzling expanse of oiled hardwood, dark and light woods fixed into a pattern of her-ringbone parquet. Immediately to our right, just an arm's length away, was a distinguished looking man, poised and proper in a black tuxe-do. Almost imperceptibly, he cleared his throat then smiled.

"Boa noite, senhoritas. Good evening. The evening is much more lovely now that you are here," he said in Portuguese.

Beyond him, we caught sight of our own faces, awestruck, reflect-ed in a mirror shimmering with the crystalline glints of wineglasses, highballs, tumblers, flutes, and snifters. Like millions of diamonds. We saw pyramids of limes and lemons, cylinders of maraschino cher-ries, jars of olives amassed on a marble counter, and decanters of liquid amber, auburn, and chartreuse assembled on glass shelving. Above the mirror, tiny stroboscopic lights blinked: On the Rocks, On the Rocks, On the Rocks. We were in a bar—not your friendly neighborhood pub—but a gleaming out-of-this-world high-class cocktail lounge on the top of an unfinished building, overlooking the city.

She had done it again, ushered us into a strange and magnificent world beyond anything we could have imagined. Like a tour guide, she pointed this way and that, zeroing in, far below, on the landmarks that we knew, giving us our bearings. We were high above Copacabana in what was obviously a five-star penthouse restaurant on the very top of an abandoned building on a derelict construction site.

We followed Ellen toward the bar. Cantilevered over the counter was a triangle of copper roofing; upright panels of glass walled in the area. But the space adjacent to the cocktail lounge had no walls, only a three-tiered guardrail running the perimeter of the floor. There, under the stars, were round tables for two, four, and eight, spread over by heavy white-on-white linens, set with white china and knives for butter, fish, and meat; forks for salads, oysters, and fruit; spoons for soup, dessert, and coffee. I had heard somewhere that you could tell a lot about a place by the weight of the silverware and the size and thickness of the napkins. This place was first class.

Most of On the Rocks was under the stars, open to the night air, but umbrellas and trees formed canopies over certain tables, and planters spilling over with flowers divided the area into quadrants. Only a few people were dining—sunset was still early for dinner by Brazilian standards—their heads drawn close in conversation. On the tables, flickering candles breathed in the night air, flaming up like tiny lungs, and fiery torches licked moonward, sizzling in an updraft.

Beyond the tables was the swimming pool, a slow undulation of shining turquoise, sparked with glints of light. Lit from within and reflecting candlelight on its shifting surface, the pool was as alive as a patch of phosphorescent sea. Only once had I seen phosphorescence.

One night, under the moon, in the San Juan Islands — the Canadian side — I had waded deeper and deeper, swishing my arms up past my elbows in the water, each gentle swipe sending dinoflagellates into a swell of luminance. I never forgot the experience, and now, again, I felt shivery and stunned by something so beautiful.

We were led to our table, waiters pulled out our chairs, and we were seated just a stone's throw from the edge. Far below us were city lights and out at sea, the once-in-awhile lights of passing ships. The moon cut a wide path on the water. Above us was the domed ceiling of inky night.

Ellen explained that ten years before, a group of entrepreneurs had planned to build a first-rate destination hotel/restaurant/bar. After completing the framework, they started at the top, intending to work their way down to the ground. Whether they ran out of money or just lost interest she didn't know, but, after the completion of On the Rocks, construction was terminated. It was as if someone had said "Freeze" and everything stayed in its place.

Backhoes, their buckets in mid-lift, stalled; steel beams lay as helter-skelter as pick-up sticks, metal filings settled like dust. But somehow — she never told us how — she found her way over the rutted lot, into the elevator cage, and up to the elegant top floor to dine under the stars.

We settled into the On the Rocks menu, selecting antipasto, butter lettuce salads, filets of beef in lemon butter, asparagus tips, wines, exotic coffees. Ellen's treat. Entranced by the view, time and time again, we blew out the candle, satisfied with the stars. But in an instant, the waiter had it relit. Finally, completely bewildered, he replaced the candle with two new ones. We gave up. Between courses, we were served palate-cleansing fruit ices and hot, moist hand towels, scented with something flowery sweet. An enchanted evening. Who back home would believe it?

On the Rocks at the top of the Panorama Palace became a regular stop on the Ellen/Karen/Lee version of the Grayline tour. Our apartment was the Grand Central Station for countless 20-something-year-olds backpacking across South America, and we were always excited to see the expressions on their faces after we pushed them onto the rickety elevator and took them up to the paradise that was On the Rocks. Never were we disappointed; every guest, including my mom, stood on the top floor, leaned over a rail, and gaped in disbelief.

MARIA ELENA

MARIA ELENA—OUR third maid, the skinny, perplexing one—lived in a favela high on the crooked spine of a mountain, a mountain the shape of a thumb, bent in the middle like an arthritic knuckle. From her shack, straight down the hillside, beyond the shops, up and over the rooftop gardens of the million-dollar high rises, the shadow-splayed lines of swaying palms, and the bright blur of four lanes of traffic were the white sands and crashing waves of the famous beach, Ipanema. Before 1964, Ipanema was famous to Cariocas; after 1964, and, now in 1969, Ipanema was famous to the world.

When composer Antonio Carlos Jobim and poet Vinicius de Moraes chose to immortalize fifteen-year-old, tall and tan, Heloísa Eneida Menezes Paes Pinto, known as "Hêlo," in the song "The Girl from Ipanema," they fashioned a fantasy. As she walked "like a samba," her swaying "more than a poem," on her way home from school, every day passing a bar in Ipanema, she made men—and women—sigh. Green-eyed Hêlo got us sighing everywhere, not just in Brazil, but also in America; even my cousins in Sweden and my friends in England knew of her. "When she passes/ each one she passes/ goes ahhh," says the song.

Even all these years later—especially on a cold Illinois day in winter—my husband will sit at the piano, play the song, and I'm back in Ipanema, my skin warm, the extra flesh of middle age fallen away from my upper arms and legs, my stomach flat and my ankles thin.

Back then, not just Hêlo caught everyone's eye—hundreds of Carioca beauties, their legs bronzed and taut, and their hips swinging, paraded along the beach, drawing out wolf-whistles and whispered suggestions. Carioca men, physically fit, their chests brown and bare, skimmed over the sand chasing soccer balls and volleyballs, leaving us to smile in our own private imaginings.

From her porch—a small 2' × 2' slab of cracked concrete and a wooden pallet with broken slats—Maria Elena's view of Rio was spectacular, tourist-brochure magnificent. But I know that she never forgot where she stood. By day, she could have looked down to the wide shoreline boulevard of people promenading up and down the wave-patterned mosaics of polished black and white rock. At night, she could have gazed at millions of lights flickering over the city and in the sky—headlights, tail lights, billboards, and stars. With just a turn of her head—sunrises and sunsets, star-splattered night skies and pale pink dawns. But my guess is she saw nothing beyond the empty shelf or the shoeless child, his nose crusted with snot and dirt. Nothing, not even this scenery—the most beautiful I had ever seen—could make Maria Elena smile. Only once had I known her to smile, really smile the tooth-wide grin of total happiness. It was when we gave her a sack of store-bought cookies, hard ginger cookies with white-squiggle frosting, to take to her three kids.

We had tried to guess her age. Small-boned and wiry, she was pencil thin, a toothpick. Her knees bowed. And the long brown toe of her left foot had pushed a hole in the tip of the white canvas slip-ons she wore everyday; her heels, like flattened potatoes, were pink and hard. From the creases on her face and the purple veins bulging from those misshapen legs, we decided that she looked forty, maybe fifty. We didn't account for the ages of her children. When she told us she was twenty-two, we gasped. Twenty-two. My age. Three kids — one was already eight. But her bent-over body told me that in ways other than years, she was old, far older than I.

I knew that there was electricity, but no running water in her favela. The people who lived there filled five-gallon olive oil cans with water from long metal troughs at the base of the mountain. We saw the favelados from the taxi as we rode through Ipanema and Copacabana to sit in air-conditioned theaters or have iced tropical juices and honey-colored *doces* — they were shaped like bird's nests and made of sugar spun into strings — downtown at Colombo's. Colombo's, the elegant colonial restaurant with walls of mirrors, where women still wore flowing, flowery, old-fashioned silk dresses — I wanted to call them "frocks" or "tea gowns," not just "dresses" — and men wore white suits and Panama hats of shaped straw.

Balancing the square gold and green cans on their shoulders, two at a time, the favelados carried the sloshing containers straight up steep wooden steps to shacks slapped together into something like a ragged, unkempt rookery, a distance of, maybe, three city blocks. I could imagine Maria Elena, wearing her faded house dress, an apron tied around her waist, carrying a single can, one hand steadying it against her head, the other hand curving protectively over her pregnant belly. I could see her climbing up the steps slowly and cautiously, a child or two grabbing at her hemline.

Somehow, one day in October, halfway up the mountain, her bare feet swollen and aching, her tired eyes closing, she missed her footing; maybe she caught a toe, misjudged a step, maybe she tripped over a child. Head over heels backwards, down a flight of stairs she fell, rolling and tumbling into a heap. Bloodied and bruised, she held back the tears, thinking — maybe hoping — she might lose the baby. Baby number four.

She was unable to work. And unable to work, she couldn't feed her children. The family lived hand to mouth. No work, no money. No money, no food. As soon as we got word of Maria Elena's accident, we asked Thereza to ask her maid Judith to take 15 contos, about $3.75 US, to her. Fifteen contos equaled pay for one and a half days of work. Hard work. Washing our towels and our jeans in a tub by hand. Hanging them to dry on the line strung between the back door and the maid's room door. Scrubbing tiled floors on her hands and knees. Scratching away at black, sticky slag stuck to the top of the stove and in the oven. Arriving early, leaving late, three days a week. Taking the stairs, three flights up. Maids were not allowed to use the elevator.

After her accident, we knew she would need help, but no one, not even Judith, would take groceries and money into the favela. Likely, someone carrying more food than for one day's meals would be beaten and robbed. The bread, eggs, and milk for Maria Elena's family would end up in someone else's twisting stomach. Survival was lawless; morality, just a word. Ellen, always invincible, convinced that luck and our foreignness could save us, decided that the three of us would take money and supplies to Maria Elena ourselves.

We arranged for Judith to escort us. She had been with Thereza's family since she was a young girl, maybe only five or six, living in a room off the balcony she shared with the Sunday chicken clucking in its wooden crate. She owned a small TV and a radio, and in her closet hung outfits for summer and winter. She returned to her family in the favela a few miles away — I thought Thereza said once a month, but maybe I misunderstood. I hope she was allowed to return at least once a week.

Mid-afternoon, before we left for the favela, I wrote a note to my mom and dad, "I can't make any sort of prejudgments — I don't know what will happen — whether I can even stand to see it. I asked

Thereza if she'd ever been to a favela. She said, 'No'; she had never even thought about it."

Probably most upper- and middle-class Cariocas felt the same way. As long as they could turn their heads from the squalor and hold their breath as they passed, the favela didn't exist. Besides, it was a scary place, with its own law, its own makeshift, self-appointed judges and juries. Gangs. Vigilantes. Warlords. A world apart. A burglary or murder in the favela wouldn't get even a sentence in the back pages of the newspaper.

Understandably, Thereza was unhappy with our decision. To set foot in the favela was comparable to pinning $100 bills and a "Mug Me!" sign to our shirts. "Louca! Insane! You're crazy. People die there. They're tied up and shot in the mouth, so their heads blow up."

Nevertheless, we packed sacks with food and boarded the bus to Ipanema. Judith was waiting for us, sitting on a bench in front of an outdoor café. We followed her up a winding dirt road, past the water troughs where people stopped the filling of their cans to stare at us.

The mountainside was plastered with shacks, thousands of them, stacked helter-skelter like blocks ready to tumble. I had heard that over 30,000 people lived here, sometimes as many as a dozen people sharing a single room. Concrete was slapped on rock, boards and a couple of bricks stuck in, planks nailed every which way, a hodge-podge, until some semblance of structure evolved. Windows were holes in the walls, places where the boards didn't meet. Roofs, tin sheets—corrugated and rusted through—randomly placed planks of wood, some painted, some not.

Continuing up the stairs, we dodged skinny, nearly naked kids, snot-nosed pigs, and feather-loose chickens. As we sidestepped and veered, Judith, in a low voice, educated us. "Where Maria Elena lives is not really a favela," she corrected us, "but a morro. Moe-whoo," she said, coaxing us to pronounce the word properly. It was a step below a favela on the social scale, for those even poorer than favelados. But the hierarchy for both the favela and the morro was the same. Location. As I looked around me, I saw what she meant. The neatest shacks, the most carefully shaped and constructed, were at the top. I realized that the farther down the mountainside I looked, the higher were the piles of garbage. There, at the base, neck high, were heaps of paper, cans, plastic, peels, and bones. Garbage everywhere, rotting and stinking. Water and sewage had seeped down from a narrow spillway at the top, widened into a muddy ditch, slogged down from the uppermost shanties to those mid-mountain, to those at the bottom, separating into shallow trenches and a pigsty of sludge, filling wheel tracks and footprints with oily green scum.

As we climbed higher, people whistled and called out to us. "Tudo bem?" "Is all well?" We laughed at the comments we'd heard a thousand times before. "How's the weather up there?" "So tall, where you from, beleza!" Men clicked their tongues and propositioned us, winking and beckoning with sensuous fingers. Judith snapped at them, and some slunk away to peek at us from behind walls. Others just laughed, making Judith scowl and hiss something untranslatable. "Idiota!" A few, only a few, eyed us suspiciously from dark doorways. Women and children said, "Olá!" Most people seemed curious. And welcoming. I wasn't scared anymore. Thereza was wrong.

On a landing, a jabbering throng of kids closed in on us, pulling on our wrists, chattering incessantly, each vying for our attention. One boy, wearing balloon shorts, chirped, "Look, look at my kite!" Another kid pushed him out of the way, yelling, "No, look at mine! I beat everyone! Look! I tied razors to my kite. I win! I win!"

On the steps, we noticed broken glass. Boys were crouched down, rolling rocks over the shards, pulverizing them into a fine powder. Judith grumbled, "These boys, naughty desordeiros, steal the light bulbs. These crazy goofball kids will cause an accident. The old men and the old ladies will trip because there is no light at their building." She cuffed a boy under his chin, "Shame on you. Somebody's grandma is going to break her leg, and you're going to cry big, big, sad tears." He just laughed and resumed rolling a rock over a light bulb.

Bare fingered, he spit into his hands and pulled the kite string meticulously through the drool, then rolled the string in the crushed glass. Finally the string was attached to the kite, and he let it go, waggling up over the shanties and the clotheslines of flapping laundry, to soar in the wind.

Against the blue sky, a dozen kites dipped and dove, bright-colored diamonds or bird shapes, like miniature condors, swooping down on other kites, kids guiding the attacks. Far off, the winning kite, an orange double-winged box with a black and purple tail, sliced through the strings of the others, sending them—even the one tied with razors—out to sea, and heavenward. The winner strutted, his thin chest puffed out with his grubby thumbs cocked in his armpits. "Cheater, cheater, cheater," yelled a kid from behind an empty garbage can. Suddenly he turned the can over and kicked it clanging down the stairs; it bounced to a stop against the closed door of a shack.

What would become of these kids? Most of them didn't go to school. Few would ever learn to read or write. Some lived on the streets, surviving by snatching food from vendors and stealing pocketbooks from old ladies. Many would die—from disease, from gang fights, from the Death Squad, the vigilante cops who took justice into their own hands. Others would make an honest living, but hardly enough to make ends meet.

The morro was noisy. Shacks were piled one on the other, sharing walls. People hung out the open windows and packed themselves onto porches. As we passed, heads turned to us and words were said, questions asked. They were polite. Who were we? Why were we here in this place? Oh, so tall! Judith kept explaining, over and over. I noticed a woman with her long black hair pulled back by a tortoise shell comb; she was humming. Another—as if she were starring in an old-fashioned movie—red, red lips and a red plastic rose pinned over her ear. Men with thick mustaches and men with mustaches so thin, they looked penciled on.

Battery-powered radios on high volume blasted music and ads, comedies, weather, and breaking news. Fuse boxes buzzed. Talking and laughing. Yelling at kids. Calling dogs. Teasing. Cajoling. Groups of people harmonized Carnaval songs, keeping the beat, drumming their fingertips on matchboxes, pots, and pans. In the favelas, on the streets, in rich neighborhoods and poor, always and everywhere in Rio, there was music. Just the Friday before, Ellen, Karen, and I had emptied the kitchen drawers and cupboards of silverware and cooking utensils and, by candlelight, with all of our friends, danced the night away to the samba rhythm of knives and spoons on colanders and kettles.

It wasn't long before we had climbed hundreds of stairs. We were panting in the late afternoon heat—like most days in Rio, dusk this day, too, was golden. The entire city and the waters of Guanabara Bay were washed with gold. We could feel pulling in our calves, feel our backs aching from the sacks of heavy cans. Because I was just coming off a month-long stay in bed with mononucleosis, I was more winded than either Karen or Ellen. My knees were weak, and I felt shaky. I stopped on a landing to rest. How many times a day did the favelados go down and up? I was exhausted. When I turned to ask the others to slow down, my breath stopped. The view was startling, magnificent. For the ten-thousandth time since arriving in Rio, I was again stunned by this city. Cidade Maravilhosa. Wonderful City. Breathtaking, beautiful.

This was Maria Elena's view, every single day. Below me, straight center was Ipanema, mottled with mosaics, black and white. To my left was Copacabana, neon-lit, bright lights bouncing. And to my right was our Leblon. I swept my eyes over modern glass buildings, pink and blue colonial mansions, open air bars with bright rainbows of umbrellas, street peddlers with plastic blow-up cartoon characters bobbling on sticks, kites and more kites swooping over the waves.

Miles and miles of dusk-tinged beaches curving into the fading bluish-gold horizon of Leme and Barra da Tijuca. Far off, I could approximate the location of our avenue, our apartment, the avocado tree outside my bedroom window, even the bakery across the street. Then I looked to my feet. I toed the pile of blackened banana peels, mold-green orange rinds, and greasy cans, uncovering a broken baby bottle, its pink nipple split like a tulip.

Finally, we reached Maria Elena's house. At the summit, it was in the "high-rent" district. To enter the house, we had to make our way through a crowd of kids, then duck under low-hanging electric lines and an off-kilter doorframe. Squinting through two windows and several narrow cracks in the walls were arrows of dust-laden yellow light. It took a second for my eyes to adjust to the dark. A mattress, a stove, a table, three chairs, and a console radio three feet long furnished the room. People—men, women, and children—stood elbow to elbow, body to body. Back against a wall sat Maria Elena, her yellow eyes vacant and dark. On the floor in front of her, we placed our sacks. Rice and black beans, oranges, a pineapple, eggs, vegetables, canned goods, aspirin. She mustered a weak smile and nodded thank you. No one said a word.

Then Ellen broke the silence. "Don't eat it all at once!" Everyone laughed, and introductions were made. First, Maria Elena's three children. Shy for a moment, then they came closer. The little girl looked up at us through spiraling curls fastened by a rainbow of plastic barrettes; the boys, their striped polo shirts buttoned to the neck, poked each other and tottered from foot to foot. I was completely taken over—they were beautiful children. But what was their future? What could I, what could we, do for them? Bring them books, teach them to read? Get them scholarships to private school? There must be something we could do.

We met Maria Elena's sister, her husband and their three kids. Maria Elena's no-account "husband," on the bare mattress, pretending to sleep, only stirred. Ten people. All of them lived in this space no bigger than my bathroom. How did they sleep, I wondered; with only enough room for five or six of them to lie down at the same time, they must have slept in a pile like puppies. Judith's two kids were there, and umpteen neighbor kids peeked in the windows and peered through the doorway. Each child was scrubbed clean, as was the house. Thereza was wrong; this place wasn't scary.

Ellen, half in Spanish, half in Portuguese, kept the conversation going. I looked around, making mental notes; I wanted, and needed, to imprint this place on my mind. Tacked to the walls, threadbare and sunbleached, were the frayed remains of futebol — soccer — banners. A 1968 calendar. Why 1968, I wondered. It was 1969, already October. But I thought better than to ask. On one wall was a mirror, about two-feet tall by three-feet wide, corroding and spotted with blotches, black and ballooning like roses. On the far wall was a wooden picture frame, glassless, a print of something — or someone — religious. Maybe macumba, or maybe Catholic, I couldn't tell, it was too faded. Black and white, scalloped-edge snapshots of the kids — celebrating birthdays, in soccer shirts, at Carnaval — were tucked haphazardly between the stained matting and the molding, nearly covering the image on the print. Tacked to the wall above the table was a picture postcard of the snake farm in São Paulo. I had been there. I recognized the snake pit. I remembered that one of the handlers had spiraled six snakes around his arm at once; I remembered the milky fangs of a snake pressed to the rim of a cup.

Maria Elena whispered something to her kids, and they turned and scampered off. In seconds, they returned. Each child held two oddly shaped, soft ball-sized wads of waxed paper. Carefully they unwrapped the packages and produced three teacups and three saucers, celadon green, almost see-through, borrowed from a neighbor. I recognized the dishes; the Supermercado Disco, the only supermarket in Leblon, was selling them — with a minimum purchase — for a few cents, a new bowl or plate each week. Occasionally we shopped at the Disco, not often, only when we were hungry for American food—Chicken-of-the-Sea or Campbell's soup—or Jell-o and instant pudding. Like Brazilians, we bought in the neighborhood from specialized shops. Our fresh fruit we bought from one of the carts pushed up and down the street, our vegetables from the stand on the corner a block away, our canned items from the shop on the ground floor of the building next to ours. We even ordered our meat from the butcher, asking for just the right cut from the fly-crusted carcass hanging on a hook in the open air.

The neighborhood vendors gave us special treatment, maybe not the celebrity status we were given at parties in upper-class Brazilian homes, but a more comfortable attention, as if we were favorite children. They fawned over us and pampered us. As we passed their stands, they called out to us, "I have saved the very best persimmon for you! Come see!" "Look at this lettuce. Not the tiniest blemish. Special for you!" "Dona Maria Santos wanted these plantains and this okra, but I say 'No! These are for the beautiful American girls.'"

Someone presented each of us with a beer. It was cold; one of the kids must have scrambled down to the bar, the botequim, below to make the purchase. The cost? A day's work. I rolled the wet, brown, long-necked bottle in my hands, waiting. For several seconds, we waited. But no more bottles appeared. Apparently only the three of us were expected to drink.

I felt awkward. I didn't want to make anyone feel bad, but I didn't want beer. Mono had kept me in bed for over a month—this was one of my first days out anywhere besides the clinic—and, doctor's orders, I had not touched alcohol, none. In fact, in my mind, I connected alcohol and mono. Karen and Ellen tipped back their bottles and drank. Nervous, imagining that my liver was shriveling into a bilious ocher mass of rot and decay, tinged in blood, I sipped, holding cold beer in my mouth, warming it, afraid to swallow. Ellen exclaimed,

"Ahhh...que deliciosa...muito obrigada...thank you, thank you!" The adults smiled, nodding at one another; they were successful hosts. I swallowed to make them feel good. The children, speaking in high-pitched English, mimicked us, "Tenka oooh," they giggled. After we finished the beer, Maria Elena's sister poured coffee from a thermos into the three green Disco cups.

We slugged down the syrupy sweet coffee in one gulp, and waited. Now what? Again I felt awkward. But Ellen quickly filled the silence with babble. The kids started to chatter, nudging each other. "Come out, come with us," they coaxed. "We show you Carnaval." Several ran out, and the adults began to stir. Within seconds, a street band was formed. Guitars, drums, pots and pans. A cassette player and a shoebox full of tapes.

Spontaneously, the floorshow began. No more talk, just music and dancing. Outside, on the front stoop of the small house and on those of the houses next door, a space about 12' × 12', the children stepped into a samba. They crisscrossed feet and knees in dance moves so complicated, I couldn't sort out their limbs. The adults sang Carnaval songs, sucked on harmonicas, beat drums, played guitars, thrummed their knuckles on the walls and doors. Spinning and whirling, the kids challenged each other to fancy footwork, each step more complex than the one before. After each performance, they looked over at us, anxious for approval. Our smiles made them wiggle in delight.

Caught up in the delirium, amazed at the precision, the balance and rhythm, Karen, Ellen, and I were spellbound. We had come for Maria Elena, but the focus was on us. This was a performance in our honor. We were celebrities, queens of the mountain.

A couple of kids pulled us into a line, we swayed into something like a mambo, and then all of us together broke into a high-kicking cancan, laughing until we doubled over. I was clicking mental pictures...remember...remember. Like pixies, the kids swarmed around us, hanging onto our waists, grabbing our hands and making us swing them in circles, their feet flying off the ground.

From somewhere, a soccer ball was thrown in, and the kids dribbled it between their feet, kicking up clouds of red dust. The ball bounced off their heads and under their legs, but they kept right on dancing. One boy yelled "Goooooaaaaaalllll!" and a bunch of kids fell into a pile laughing, shrieking, untangling themselves and dancing again. Their faces gleamed, and their little legs were dusted red, like knee socks.

Finally, Maria Elena stepped in and touched the children lightly on their heads. "Chega!" (Enough!) They backed over to a wall, slid down to a sitting position—a line of six or eight of them, chins and elbows resting on their knees. Karen, Ellen, and I followed her back into the house. She handed me a gray plastic View Master, the kind I'd had as a kid. "Olha." Holding it to the light, I clicked through the cardboard photo rings of children, the six cousins, Maria Elena's and her sister's kids, big eyed and smiling. The girls, their pigtails tied with white ribbons, wearing identical white dresses with pearl buttons and ruffled collars. Maria Elena's boys, barefooted, in black and red striped soccer shirts, waving black and red flags for their favorite futebol team, Flamengo. Her sister's boys in maroon and green, the colors of Fluminence. "Fla" and "Flu." Enemy teams. Where would these kids be in ten years? I wondered. In twenty?

I passed the View Master to Ellen. "Hey, how come you guys are wearing soccer shirts from Chile?" she teased. Immediately the boys were in her face, shaking their heads, but, a second later, they were back to arguing about scores, swearing that Flamengo's goalie was garbage, and Fluminence's sweeper was a million trillion times better than Flamengo's, and vice versa. Laughing, Ellen winked at Karen and me, and we started to chant, "USA, USA!" Hands pawed at our ribs, trying to pull up to our mouths to muffle our words. Ellen threw back her head and yelled, "Pelé, Pelé, Pelé!" and all the kids dropped down, joined in, turning, clapping, and jumping. "Pelé, Pelé!" Their hero. Our hero. The king of soccer. And we were all together again.

It was getting late. The sun had set, and the morro flickered with lanterns, lamps, and candles. A man came into the room, the contours of his face reflected in the dim light. There was something menacing about the curve of his eyebrows and the sharpness of his jaw. He was eating chunks of potatoes, still in their skins, from a greasy sack. His teeth were yellow, and he was missing an eyetooth. Suddenly he grabbed a kid by the scruff of his neck, turned him around, snapped his rear end with a thumb and an index finger, and roared, "Get home to your mama! Now!" The little boy scampered to the door, bent over, wiggled his behind at the man, and ran off into the night. The man laughed, and said, "What a boy! You wait and see, he'll make something of himself!"

Judith introduced us to him. João was his name. He wore a white shirt, unbuttoned from neck to waist, dingy sleeves rolled up over his elbows, khaki shorts, and lace-up boots. Hanging from his belt was a leather-sheathed knife. Then I began to understand. He was our bodyguard for the trip back down the stairs in the dark.

I stood in the doorway and looked again at the room. A single light bulb bobbled on a cord looped over a hook screwed to the ceiling. A blue rubber elephant that squeaked. A blue plastic tommy gun on the wooden floor. And over the stove, on a nail, a pink plastic heart filled with red-tipped kitchen matches. My last vision of Maria Elena's house was of a gun and a heart.

We hugged Maria Elena—she was thinner than I had thought—and told her we'd be back. Soon. The children followed us down the stairs until Judith shooed them away. "Don't leave, Miss Ellen, don't leave, stay with us, come back, Miss Karen, stay, Miss Lee," they cried. Maria Elena's sister walked down a few flights with us. Someone's baby, not hers, clung to her side, his feet wrapped tight around her belly. Part way down, she kissed our cheeks and said, "Thank you. Heaven will look down on you."

As we descended, João announced us. "Step aside," he said. "Ladies coming through." Someone offered us a lit candle. "Take care." "Have a good night," they said.

We thanked Judith, and she put us on the bus. Through the dusty window, I looked at her and João. They smiled and waved. As João backed toward a streetlight, I saw a silver flash. Under his unbuttoned shirt, tucked in his waistband was a gun. Maybe, after all, Thereza was right.

Maria Elena didn't come back to work, and we didn't make it back to the morro. So I never learned from her what I sensed she knew. But I thought often about her and her children, and all of the others. They were happy the day I met them; for a few hours, they were happy. And so were we.

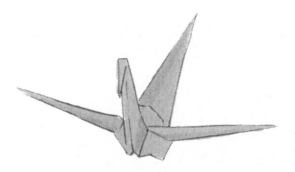

THE NIGHT OF NIGHTS

FOR WEEKS, I LOOKED forward to New Year's Eve. Looked forward? Definitely an understatement. I could hardly wait. For believers of macumba, this was the night of nights. How would the events on the stretch of beach from Leblon to Ipanema to Copacabana compare to what I knew of religion? In Rio, of course, I was never too far from religion — right out my window, high on the mountain, his feet rising out of the billowing mist, was Corcovado, Christ the Redeemer. And hardly ever did we leave the apartment without seeing something of macumba — a circle of candles, a hair twisted on a doorknob, someone with a fingernail an inch long.

About 11 p.m., we got into the elevator and broke out onto the street. I paired up with John, my freckle-faced, tousle-haired friend whom I'd known at the University of Washington. He was in Rio trying to find a job after abruptly leaving the Peace Corps. He had come to Brazil with high hopes, but, after a few months, his tour ended badly. I never knew the whole story. He was always cleaning his Coke-bottle-thick lenses and grinning. Without his glasses, his eyes looked like underwater-sea-creature eyes, blurry and unfocused.

John and I went south. At first, I was wide-eyed fascinated, then dazzled, completely in awe. Above us, stars and the moon pinpricked the black sky. Before us in the sand were thousands and thousands of candles. White candles. Placed in configurations of crosses, circles, or squares. A giant chalice. A crown of thorns. I could squint the flames together into serpentines of light, strings of calligraphy angling and looping through the dark.

Like my woodsy places back home, the sand was swept smooth, mounded by hand into sacred shapes. Crowding over the flames were black faces, heads wrapped in white sheeting, eyes lit bright. As far as I could see, from the twin cliffs of Dois Irmãos back to the bend at Ipanema, patterns waggled over the beaches like a blazing marquee, celebrating this night of heaven on earth. Some altars were so near the water's edge that the waves lapped the Atlantic into the candle-filled trenches, reflecting four- and five-fold the millions of flickers quivering in the night. Others bounced light off the glass fronts of buildings, jewelling the night with a zillion sparks of bright confetti.

I had read that over a million people—those who believed in macumba and those who came to watch—made their way to the beaches lining the Rio coast. And here we were—John and I, thousands of miles from our own homes—with them, between the sea and the street in a sea of people. We didn't talk; we watched and walked.

The celebrants wore white—white wrappings on their heads, white blouses and skirts, shirts and pants. Feet were bare. Occasionally someone passed by wearing an open-necked shirt or a long flowing skirt of pink or blue. But mostly we saw white. In their arms, they carried flowers—long stems of white or apricot-colored gladioli, pale roses, or sprigs of orange blossoms.

Thick with the smell of flowers and of incense—frangipani, eucalyptus, patchouli—the air was wet. Tropical, warm. At some shrines, drums throbbed; at others, men and women in locked arms wailed or chanted or sang. Many danced in slow rotating circles. Smoke from candles and small fires wound through the crowds, diaphanous garlands connecting us one to the other.

A small boy—like John, a real grinner—snatched my hand and gently pulled me down toward his face. He whispered Portuguese in my ear, "You are pretty, lady." I grinned, but I'd been in Rio long enough to know that anyone with light skin was pretty. Despite what the travel brochures said about Brazil being "colorblind," color mattered.

I sat in the sand next to him as his two sisters bent to kiss each of my cheeks. One smiled shyly and said, "Tonight Iemanjá will touch your face." John squatted beside me, and they lifted his face with their tiny brown hands and kissed his cheeks. Their altar of sand was sculpted into two interlocking rings, scooped and mounded two yards or more across. In the center of each ring a white lace cloth was spread. In one ring, dug into the sand, were two pictures, gold-framed, one of Mary and one of Jesus. In the second ring, much larger than Mary and Jesus, framed in gold filigree, was the portrait of Iemanjá, the white-skinned, raven-haired goddess of the waters, her ice-blue gown growing out of the sea. Black-skinned mothers, fathers, and children bowed before the white-skinned beauty.

On this, Iemanjá's night of nights, over a million people would gather on the beach to pay homage; they would present her with trinkets and delicacies. In exchange, over the next year, she would provide for them voluminous nets, dripping and spilling over with flopping fish. She, the supreme protector, would keep their men safe on the seas—fathers, husbands, and sons.

To please the goddess, this family had fashioned a dressing table, a vanity of feminine luxuries. Carefully they had arranged lipstick, rouge, silver-cased powders, and glass-bottled perfumes on a large hexagonal mirror, its edges beveled in serrated scallops. I thought of home—of the perfume counter at the dime store, blue bottles of Evening in Paris, my woodland shrines. The boy offered a handful of rose petals to John and me and nudged us to scatter them over the sand, and we did.

"We come from Bahia, many, many miles from here," the boy said. I nodded. I knew Bahia. I hadn't been there, but when my friend Dick spoke of it, he smiled as if he were seeing some beatific vision. "Bahia is Brazil, heart and soul. Real Brazil. There, macumba is called Candomblé. It's primitive, close to its African roots — so much more authentic, so true to its origin. You haven't been to Brazil until you've been to Bahia." Someday I would go there.

"Our father, one year ago, passed on," the boy said. "We come here, his birth home, to bless his spirit and the spirit of his mother."

The boy again took my hand and led me away, taking me through the haze of candle smoke, around collections of humanity. Finally he stopped, looked up at me, and nodded once as if to say, "This is it!"

Fifty people, maybe more, were in a long, loosely formed line, swaying to the drums like a Chinese dragon. At the head of the line, slowly turning, then spinning wildly, was a woman. By her appearance, I knew she was a Mãe de Santo, a high priestess.

"She is a special one who can speak in my father's voice. She comes here tonight from Bahia, like us," the boy said. "You must speak with her, too."

We walked closer to her. Moving constantly, she hopped in circles from right to left, then left to right, her bare feet flying over the sand. The flab on her arms jiggled and her heavy breasts flopped. I was confused by my impression of her — she was clownish, even grotesque, but strangely regal. Something about her compelled me, drew me to her.

Dressed head to toe in white with strands and strands of beads slapping against her chest, she must have weighed over 350 pounds, but she was light on her feet, almost delicate. She was short, shaped like a box, but her headdress of feathers was at least three feet tall, and, when she stood still for a minute or two, she seemed statuesque, like an African goddess carved from the trunk of an exotic tree.

She sucked on a fat cigar, expelling round puffs of smoke from one side of her mouth then the other. We moved back from her, and John pushed me into the line, next to a family of favelados — a father, a mother, and four little ones. Immediately, they broke into a samba, circling around me, clapping and crooning a frenzied Carnaval song. Suddenly they stopped dead still, quivered like tuning forks, and broke into wild jigging and bobbing, crisscrossing their feet, scissor stepping faster than whirlwinds. Round and round they spun, the children shrieking and squealing. I stood, quiet, in the middle, feeling awkward. I had been born with no rhythm, no voice.

The boy pulled me down and whispered, "That Mãe, she is blessed by many gods. She can make roses out of air. Once my sister saw her make the roses. Yellow roses. Seven roses at one time."

The favelados completed their dance, and the long line kept moving. One after the other, Mãe blessed the believers, sending some off with smiles and others in tears. Finally in front of her, I was eye to eye with the tickling green, yellow, and red feathers of unrecognizable tropical birds. I stooped, and, with the cigar between her middle finger and her ring finger, she managed somehow to grab my shoulders, ashes spiraling down onto my arm. She pushed her oily black face into my cheeks, kissing me on both sides of my mouth. That close, I could feel a wiry chin hair brush my lip.

"One, two, three," she counted. "Yes, twenty eight, your lucky number. And seven." How did she know that, I wondered.

She turned me around, and, still holding the cigar, jerked my shoulders, and ran her fingers up and down my spine as if I were a piano, thumping some vertebrae, caressing others. Turning me around again, she rested her hands on my shoulders, then smoothed her hands down my arms. By now, the cigar was back between her wet lips, smack in the middle of her puckered mouth. She took a deep breath in, raised up my arms, and spewed thick swirls of smoke into my armpits.

"In the name of the Father, the Son, and the Holy Ghost, bless you.

You are something…something…something…I couldn't make out the words…and your year will be wondrous and bright,"I thought she said, the words forming in the space around the cigar. Her words continued, guttural and moaning, but I couldn't translate; I didn't know when one word ended and another began. I tried to speak, but my words disintegrated in the din of drums and pounding surf.

I stumbled away, only to be caught by a Pai de Santo, a male priest, who raised my arms and whirled me around and around and around, blowing smoke rings in my armpits with each rotation.

"Spin and spin and spin,"he chanted. ""Lambs and birds and…"he seemed to be saying.

Crowds of faces smeared into an orbit of blur, like swaths of paint spun off a brush. After half a dozen turns, he stood me square in front of him. Muttering, he scribbled his fingers down my arms and grabbed my little fingers, jerking and pulling. Each finger he tugged and snapped.

Then, looking directly into my eyes, he said, "John, your friend, he is in danger. He is here, in Brazil, because Vietnam is bad, very bad. But he is in big danger in America. He should go far away to Africa." Then his words became garbled, and I couldn't understand; he swung me away by my wrists, saying, "You, yes, you will return to America."

I was confused. How on earth did he know John's name? How did he know John had come to Brazil to escape the draft? How…? I tried to tell John what the Pai had said, but drums and noise, singing and chanting made communication impossible. I pulled John to me and screamed in his ear. He just grinned and nodded. I was baffled.

By midnight, the tempo of the night had quickened; songs and dances now seemed electric-charged, sizzling. The beat swelled to fever pitch. Around me, people shook, trembled, and retched. They stiffened and threw themselves to the ground, thrashing and rolling in the sand, their eyes bulging out of the sockets. They wailed and yipped like animals, hissing and whinnying, their cries agonizing as death. "Take me, take me, Iemanjá, take me. Bless me. I beseech you, take me."

In trances, some seemed almost to be lifted to the water, as if they were caught in a spell, drawn headlong into the foaming blackened waves. Transfixed, they moved forward, ankles, knees, hips, while others wrestled with them, clawing at them, screamed for them to turn back, terrified that they'd be sucked into the undertow and drowned. Dragged back, they convulsed and collapsed. Then they slept, fixed to the sand, almost dead, unmoving. Finally, pitching forward and back, they stood clumsily, righting themselves to full height.

On every face was the same look. Innocence. Peace. Tranquility. What had seemed frightening, even ugly, was replaced by a look of deep benevolence, of grace. It was as if hundreds of Mother Marys and Jesus Christs—a Mary or a Jesus I might have imagined as a child, soft and glowing—had touched onto shore, their bodies weightless above the sand, and their faces like child faces, unlined and dreamy.

At midnight, the crowds moved closer to the water's edge. A girl handed me a bundle of gladiolas. "Please have them," she said. As I touched the flowers, I felt a surge from head to toe. A shiver. Around me, chanting men, women, and children were breaking from the crowd and wading in, their voices rising and falling with the breaking surf. They carried blue painted boats two or three feet long, the decks glittering with candles. Deeper and deeper they went, in past their knees, past their waists, finally settling the boats gently on rolling waves. Others, hundreds of them, entered the water with armloads of flowers tied with ribbons, laying the bundles among the glowing boats.

Following them, water over my knees, I dropped my flowers into the waves and watched them scatter. I caught my breath; no longer was I invisible, no longer just an observer. I felt connected, a part of something miraculous. Water snaked up my legs, and I let my fingers fall into the surf. Water. Ablution.

Then, over Ipanema, the skies exploded with fireworks. The

cosmos was spinning; giant pinwheels of fantastic colors burst and swirled over the candle-boats rocking on the tide. With each burst, the crowd held a collective breath, and their breath was my breath. Then, between firings, we whispered and pointed at the boats, and crossed our fingers. We prayed. If Iemanjá was pleased with our gifts, she would accept them graciously and permit the boats to float out to sea; if she found the gifts faulty, unworthy, she would toss them upside down, topsy-turvy, candles doused, back to shore. And the sea would be cursed for one full year. On this night, the last of 1969, just past midnight, the little blue boats floated—floated farther and farther away until they were only bright sparks in the night, until they were gone.

I sat down in the sand, spent, as if I'd been snapped away from the cosmos. John sat beside me, his arm around my shoulder. For a long time we sat, speechless.

❧

EARLY MORNING AFTER MIDNIGHT we caught a bus to Copacabana. Parked along Avenida Atlântica were hotel vans and tourist buses. Guides with megaphones explained in English and German and French to groups of Americans and Europeans what was occurring. "Get your souvenirs here! Iemanjá statues! Iemanjá necklaces! Buy coconut cookies here! Brought in today from Bahia, fresh today!"

No fat Mães de Santo danced over the sand in Copacabana. Only young, thin glamour girls dressed in skimpy white gowns, with movie star lips, and top heavy with hair. No cigars. No chin hair or moles or sweat. No trances, no wailing, no eyes rolling in their sockets or mouths foaming. Instead, sleek, long-legged bronze beauties, nearly naked, their faces painted with Carnaval glitter, flowers in their glorious hair, titillating the crowds. They could shake their sequined nipples and bikinied behinds like jack hammers.

Up and down the beach, dancers in open shirts and skirts of red, purple, and green gyrated to the split-second beat of Carnaval sambas. They were costumed. Choreographed. Like characters in a movie. Scripted. Professional dance troupe perfect. Drummers, too, were dressed alike. They pounded on their drums, flipped their drumsticks in unison and, synchronized, clapped their hands, over their heads. After each set, they shuffled through sheet music to see what song was next. Vendors hawked souvenirs — chains with metal Iemanjá and fish charms, balloons, plastic flowers. We watched the performance as kids begged, pulled on shirt sleeves, and promised that they could lead the turistas to the "Best Macumba Show" ever. The air was sweet with the smell of peanuts and sugar turning on wooden spades in huge copper pans over fires, the prices twice that of any ordinary day.

A boy walked up to me. In Portuguese, he asked, "You speak French?" I smiled, and shook my head no. "Where you from?" John stepped in, and the guessing game began. Soon at least a half dozen little boys surrounded us, asking questions a mile a minute.

"Lady, you got to be from Sweden or Denmark where the little mermaid is. You're like the stewardesses from the airplanes from Copenhagen. You're tall and light. Look at your yellow hair. Where's the guy from?"

John teased them, telling them he was Japanese, then Mongolian, Icelandic, yes, Icelandic. When he finally admitted to them that we were Americans, the kids couldn't believe it. "Nah, man, you don't talk Portuguese like an American, all coming out your nose. You've got to be lying."

I apologized for my less-than-perfect Portuguese, but one boy pulled on my elbow, winked, and said, "Your accent is groo-ooovy." The English word sent them into fits of laughter, poking and jabbing one another in the ribs.

"Sua nome, sua nome?" When I answered that my name was Lee, they pointed to the labels on their cut-off blue jeans. "Lee jeans, you Lee jeans!" I tried to explain that no, I didn't have anything to do with Lee jeans, but they were hooting and hollering in excitement, refusing to believe anything but that I was the Lee of Lee jeans. That gave way to shouting for their favorite samba school, their favorite futebol team, their favorite brand of soccer ball. One boy checked his watch, yelled that they needed to get going, and two boys, walking backwards and waving, told us to meet them tomorrow—their families were having a New Year's Day party, and we were invited. Avenida Nossa Senhora Copacabana. Mid-day. Come, be sure to come!

We rode the bus back to Leblon. For an hour or so, we sat wordless on the beach in the black, star-studded amphitheatre of the universe. The dancing was no longer wild and frenetic, but slow and dreamy; no longer were the drums beating crazy; we listened to guitars and soft singing. People were quiet, waiting. More tiny boats, candles fixed to their decks, were dropped into the water and carried out to the sea. Again, I remembered phosphorescence, how once I had dipped my hands into slow curling waves, lighting the surface to shimmering. Not even that memory could compare with this night. I felt as if I were touched and touching, connected to everyone and to everything by invisible, weightless silken threads. Here, I was a part of the steady pulse of the cosmos. Here, I could breathe. And I felt warm.

Dawn came up deep red, orange, pink, purple, then green and yellow, unlike any sunrise I had ever seen. The waves and sand turned golden, and everyone on the beach wandered off in different directions. Still wordless, John and I walked back to the apartment. Karen was in the kitchen squeezing oranges into juice, pulling coffee cakes from the oven, scrambling eggs, and cutting pineapple into boats. By all appearances, it was a morning like so many others. But nothing, nothing at all, was ordinary about how I felt. Words didn't exist, yet, to describe my feelings, but I knew something deep inside me had been touched, and I felt peace, at ease with the inexpressible mystery of creation.

John hugged me, and left. Wordless.

I walked down the hallway to my bedroom, lay eyes closed, but sleepless, on my bed. I had left the domed dark theatre of the night world, knowing that I had been the audience and the actor, a bit part, but nonetheless, an actor, changed and changing. After replaying the scenes again and again, I felt the flap at the end of the film in my mind, and I slept. Peacefully and deeply.

CHILDREN OF THE STREETS

João WAS FOURTEEN OR fifteen—he didn't know for sure—he told us he'd been on his own ever since he could remember. He lived on the streets, sleeping in entryways and stairwells. I kept trying to convince him to go to school, to learn to read and write—I even imagined some Horatio Alger success story, our photos—my white face and his black one—in a full-color spread in Manchete or Brazilian Time. But he laughed at me and pulled a wad of money out of his pocket.

"I do okay, I do okay, better than okay," he said, winking at me.

The kid was sharp as a tack. He had picked up English from American sailors and stood ready on the dock whenever navy ships came into port. I was sure he could cuss like a seaman, but not when he spoke to us. He was a gentleman, a gentle boy.

In the grimy pocket of his khaki shorts, he kept a spiral flip pad of schedules, names, and appointments, recorded in a cryptic scrawl of his own creation. For a fistful of American dollars, he could show swabbies "a real good time," he told us. He knew lots of "good" girls, and he could mix a better-than-good batida, "the crash," a drink made of fermented sugar cane juice that went down easy and hatched a headache that left homesick sailors blind as bats.

Once I gave him a handful of cruzeiros to buy me a stash—no doctors needed, we made our own diagnoses—of parasite pills, the Pepto-Bismol pink ones. But I never saw him again.

João was only one of thousands of Brazilian kids fending for themselves. Daily they pulled on our shirtsleeves with scabby hands, begging for coins or cigarettes. Some snatched billfolds and purses from tourists. Others swiped stuff from shops and ate garbage in alleys. I knew that some parents broke the bones of their children on purpose. Some purposely pushed dirt into the sores on their kids' faces, arms, and legs; they picked off the scabs and scraped the lesions with used razors or dirty forks until the wound was bloody and filled with pus. The uglier, the better. A maimed child could beg, he could survive, he could support his family. Many families made a more-than-adequate living by begging. Certain streets and corners were even prime real estate, perfect for bumming money from strangers; these profit-rich sites were fought for, won and lost, bought and sold.

Life on the streets had its own law and order, and street children knew they wouldn't live much past seventeen or eighteen. They expected to be killed by gangs or by the Death Squad, off-duty cops who supplemented their legitimate income by trafficking drugs or pocketing cash for protection. I heard that sometimes cops killed kids who knew too much, and sometimes they killed kids because kids were the competition.

At school, our kids taunted each other, "Better do as I say, or I'll send the Esquadrao da Morte after you!" The seventh graders especially would group around my desk and yammer on and on about the Death Squad.

"Miss Lee, Miss Lee, you won't believe it, but it's true, I know this for sure. My cousin told me that his maid told him that the Esquadrao da Morte came to the favela last night. They took away the man—the skinny one with the ear that looks like a dog chewed on it—he's the man who shines shoes at Praça General Osorio. They took him to the mountain and tore off his clothes and tied him with ropes and taped his mouth and eyes shut. They cut off his fingers and his lips. They cut off his lips! They tortured him and tortured him until he died. They pinned a note to him—they pinned it right in his stomach—that said 'I sold marijuana.' And at the bottom of the note was a skull and crossbones and it was signed E.M. They brought the body back to the favela and put it where everybody gets their water. Everybody went to get water this morning, and there was the shoeshine man without his lips and no fingers. Miss Lee, my cousin said it's really for true."

"And Miss Lee, my gardener told me that the Esquadrao da Morte has a PR man, and he's called Rosa Vermelha—that means Red Rose—because blood makes a flower like a rose around a bullet hole. Rosa Vermelha tells the newspaper where they can find the bodies of the people the Esquadro kills. A presunto—that's a ham—is a white man and a chouriço—a smoked sausage—is a black man. The Esquadro kills the bad people, but my daddy says the Esquadro is bad, too."

The Death Squad meted out punishment as they saw fit. Their targets were petty thieves—pickpockets, druggies, lifelong criminals with rap sheets of minor offenses a mile long. No judge, no trial, no jury. Get the riffraff off the streets and save the taxpayers some money. The public seemed to turn a blind eye.

BEAUTY

WHEN I FIRST ARRIVED in Brazil, I was taken aback by what seemed to be the inordinate attention of Brazilians to physical appearance. On the streets of Leblon or Ipanema or Copacabana, it was often hard to tell a high-society jet setter from a domestic. Manicurists traded skills with seamstresses who traded skills with hairdressers. Rio women somehow managed to look as if they had just stepped away from a photo shoot. Not just aging matrons, but thirty-something-year-olds slapped down cruzeiro after cruzeiro for eye lifts, tummy tucks, and breast augmentations. In Copacabana, it was easier to find a cosmetic surgeon than an internist. Beautiful bodies weren't just found on travel brochures and in fashion magazines, they were everywhere.

Quickly, I learned that although we Americans went to the beach to take in the sun and swim in the surf, Cariocas went to be seen. They didn't throw down a blanket and lie in the sun; instead, they stood, moving with the sun, like a rotisserie, tanning their bodies evenly. Both women and men preened and paraded, creating on the beaches a mega-sized singles club of "the beautiful people."

Stateside, I'd been schooled to believe in "inner beauty" and that "true beauty is more than skin deep." In fact, spending time on things of the body — cosmetics, primping, bubble baths — made me feel guilty. It was a self-imposed guilt, origin unknown. Years before, I had wanted to wear makeup to cover a giant junior high pimple, but I was much too embarrassed to ask my mom — I don't know why — probably she would have told me I didn't need it, but, if that's what I wanted, okay. One morning, before school, I smeared thick orange-pink calamine lotion down my nose and over my cheeks; I must have looked like a creature done up with pumpkin rot, but I couldn't bring myself to ask for real makeup, and mom didn't even lift an eyebrow when she saw me.

In Brazil, far away from home, I was allowing myself to experiment, and Karen, with her Southern ways, was teaching me to embrace things luxurious and feminine. I was learning to pamper my body. The very first session with the masseuse — lazing under thrumming fingers rolling over my skin and the warmth of body wraps and exfoliates — hooked me. After twenty-one years of covering myself with heavy clothing and concentrating on the mind and not the body, I was finding that something about skimpy halter-tops and bikinis was liberating.

Carefully but slowly, I was trying to peel away some of the restraints of my old-school Scandinavian heritage. By the early 1960s, my Swedish cousins were already living in sin and going naked on the beaches of the Baltic, but I was still being raised "Old Country." I was a good girl. With every choice I made, I could feel my Grandma Isaacson, from the southern tip of Sweden, pinching at my shoulders, scolding, whispering "No" in my ears, and stepping back to look at me with steel-gray eyes. "Be a good girl, Lee Ann." Friends ribbed me for trying to be "too perfect." "Quit trying to be the social conscience of the county," they said. "Live a little!" I was still trying to satisfy the "shoulds," but, in Brazil, I was beginning to broaden the boundaries.

Easter at Ouro Prêto

THE THREE OF US—a girl named Susan (she moved in with us after Ellen resigned and returned to the States), Karen, and me—left Rio at ten on Wednesday night, headed for Ouro Prêto, an historic mountain town in the state of Minas Gerais. The roads were hazardous—short stretches of pavement and long stretches of dirt and gravel. Even two decades later when Brazil would be crisscrossed by over 990,000 miles of roads, only nine per cent would be paved. And, typically, Brazilian bus drivers were hell bent on defying physics. Ours was no different—he flew off the blacktop into ruts and potholes, bouncing the bus like a beach ball.

He dropped us off at Praça Tiradentes in the center of Ouro Prêto. Every Brazilian town has its own Tiradentes something-or-other—a square, a plaza, a street, or a corner. We circled our gaze…stucco buildings, white, pink, blue, and yellow with red-orange tile roofs…cobblestone streets…heavy doors intricately carved…frescoes of bulbous garlands of fruit…pop-eyed gargoyles and cherubs. Churches, churches, and more churches. Not even churches actually, but cathedrals aimed skyward with hand-carved spires and elaborate baroque steeples.

Horse-drawn carts bumped along the road interspersed with cars and bicycles. Tied to a post right in the center of town was a mule, hang-headed and sullen. Strapped to its saddle were two white chickens — live chickens, flapping and squawking. These were Easter dinner chickens, not chickens to be carried in a burlap bag up a jungle trail to a hidden fire pit to have their eyes picked out.

We lifted our suitcases and headed on foot for Rua Brigadeiro Musqueira 6. Pouso do Chico Rei, our hotel.

We had visited Ouro Prêto once before at the insistence of some of Susan's Brazilian friends. Before coming to Rio, she had worked in New York City as a personnel manager at Sloan-Kettering Cancer Center. There she met Senhor Aldo Cavallo, an elderly Brazilian of Italian descent, who was undergoing treatment. Like any proper Carioca, he invited her to Rio where he introduced her to his niece Vera who, in turn, introduced her to a fascinating group of women. In no time, Susan came to realize that Vera and her friends were not just ordinary folks; they were the Brazilian literati, elite women of remarkable talent and reputation. Authors, musicians, songwriters, and performers, some were on the cutting edge of a new, but largely underground, Brazilian feminist awareness, and others, Vera included, were "take-on-the-world, no-holds-barred" out-of-the-closet lesbians ready to change the world.

None of us had known women like them before. Primarily through Susan, but occasionally on my own, I peeked into their lives of fame and fortune and also into their intimate relationships. One minute they were engaged in cerebral conversation, discussing politics, literature, or religion, and the next, they were squabbling with one another, switching partners in on-again, off-again liaisons, causing us to grit our teeth and shake our heads.

"I had no idea women could be so complicated," Susan sighed. "They're absolutely amazing. So challenging but so, so, so frustrating. Thank god I like men—men are a whole lot simpler."

It was Vera who suggested that we visit Ouro Prêto. She said we would stay at Pouso Chico Rei, the small—only five rooms—hotel owned by her good friend Lilli Correia de Araújo.

Out of earshot, Susan whispered, "I've heard that Lilli gave up men after Pedro died. Women only. 'To preserve his memory' she says. I guess, to each her own!"

We finished the steep uphill hike from Praça Tiradentes to the familiar porch outside Lilli's door. She met us with open arms. We exchanged hugs and the obligatory brush and peck to each cheek, and she explained that we'd be sharing the hotel with some young gentlemen—a traveling drama troupe. She pointed down the hall, and we could see them in the dining room, scrawny and unkempt, sprawled on the delicate caned and upholstered chairs.

Some were reading, some were plucking on guitars, and some were just sitting around, looking sleepy. Untidy and pale, they were different from us. We were tired, but we were clean. And like real Cariocas, our nails, both fingers and toes, were manicured and polished. Our clothing was pressed. In contrast, they looked pale, underfed, and scruffy. We had assimilated Carioca custom and culture, devoting hours to body sculpting, weekly pedicures, and golden tans. Obviously, they were from somewhere else.

On Thursday, Friday, and Saturday, we shopped and visited tourist sites, moving from one baroque architectural wonder to the next. One night, we returned to Calabouça for dinner and a chat with the bartender, followed by cracking open a couple of bottles of wine back at Lilli's, and listening to the drama boys playing guitars and harmonicas until 5 am. Then, on Sunday morning, an hour after a gray-green dawn, we rolled out of bed, ready to see why Vera had said we must spend Easter in Ouro Prêto. Easter. Certainly a loaded word—charged with mystery and metaphor. We were ready to embrace another new

163

experience. I opened the front door and, in an instant, I knew what she meant. Newly whitewashed cobblestones were covered in flower petals, and scrambling this way and that were dozens of tiny angels.

The angels were real. Almost. All the little girls of the town — brown, black, white, and shades of coffee with cream — were dressed in white satin gowns, wings of goose feathers fastened to their tiny backs and tinsel halos pinned into their hair. All the little boys, shepherd's staffs in their fists, wore blue or beige, and their heads were bound in turbans wrapped tight over flapping colored fabric. In this shapeless parade, the children ran and skipped, and, then, for a few minutes, reined in by a parent or a tut-tutting nun, they walked sedately, eyes fixed ahead, solemn. But soon, like a scattering of birds, they were off again, whirling and twirling, preening and pecking.

During the night, priests and penitents on hands and knees had slopped water onto the streets and scoured them with scrub brushes and brooms. The cobblestones were painted white, then sawdust and flower petals—roses and carnations, mountain wildflowers — were carefully arranged into crosses and thorny crowns, candelabra, hands praying, symbols for alpha and omega. Some children, cautious, sidestepped the designs, but others tore pell-mell through the petals, sending up a clutter of color — pink, green, crimson, and gold.

Hundreds of people lined the streets to watch the procession of angels and shepherds. On both sides of the street, porches spilled over with humanity—legs poked through black wrought-iron railings and arms wrapped around spindle rods patterned with filigree. Hanging from second- and third-story balconies — wide enough for only two or three people — townsfolk waved and whistled, sang out to the children, not in the Carioca Portuguese of Rio, but in the accent of the mountain inland. "Terezinha, fix your wings! They're crooked, silly girl. Smile!" "Tonio, you have feathers in your hair! Que abacaxi!" Literally, "What a pineapple!" but slang for "What a prickly mess!"

The three of us joined the joggling throng, and the procession moved through town like a giant amorphous creature, shot through with flame flickers of candlelight and smoke smudges from incense burners swinging from the hands of white-robed priests. From cathedral to cathedral, we pushed forward, swaying with hymns sung a cappella, moving to what seemed almost a bossa nova beat.

For centuries, Lilli told us, the people of Ouro Prêto had observed Easter this way. In fact, with processions of angels and shepherds, and millions of lighted candles, they celebrated a number of saints' days, thanking God for their multitudes of good fortune. During the early days of the 1700s, men had unearthed gemstones and panned rivers for gold; they had bored the mountains for diamonds, tourmalines, aquamarines, topaz, and emeralds, and had raked them in by the ton. Beyond their wildest dreams, they became rich. Vila Rica. Rich Village. Thankful, they built thirteen cathedrals, magnificent baroque monstrosities, to honor God. Now, on holy days, their descendants, no longer rich in most cases, kept the rituals, winding from church to church, singing praises, leaving lit candles everywhere, on steps, balustrades, and curbs.

Mid-morning, the procession wound its way to the doors of the thirteenth cathedral. The crowd dispersed, and Susan and Karen wandered off to take pictures. I sat alone on the steps of the church. Three tiny angels, their halos askew and their wings lopsided and drooping, came toward me and sat down, two on one side of me and one on the other.

"Hi, angels, is this your church?" I asked. "Are you friends?"

"Uh huh," nodded one. "And we're best friends and cousins."

One little girl was black, one was white, and one was some exotic shade in between, but most likely they actually were cousins, a ménage of color. The black girl, the smallest, was like the beggar kids we had met in Bahia — her eyes, startling, were emerald green, and her curls were burnished with gold. She smiled shyly at me, snatched a feather from her wing and placed it behind my ear. Giggling they ran off

165

to who knows where. They were only four- or five-years-old at most, but no mom or dad was anywhere near.

After the Easter parade disbanded, Karen, Susan, and I wandered back to the inn.

"Are the drama boys sleeping through Easter?" I asked Lilli. "They missed all the excitement. The procession was amazing, just fantastic. Vera is right. Everyone should spend Easter here at least once in their life."

"They're gone," she said. "Maybe Julian is taking them to São Paulo. They're doing a production sometime, I think, of Jean Genet's The Balcony. They'll be gone for a couple of weeks, but they'll be back."

Something stirred in my head. "Who?" I asked.

"Julian Beck. The Living Theatre."

I nearly dropped my cup of coffee.

Senior year, my English teacher Anne McCracken had introduced me to the Living Theatre. One day she brought an armload of plays into class—plays from the ancient Greeks, Shakespeare, centuries of plays, even contemporary plays from the theater of the absurd. Also, she dumped a stack of magazines from a grocery sack onto her desk and held up a copy of *The New Yorker*. "Go to the theater review section," she said. "See what's playing on Broadway, off-Broadway, and off-off Broadway. Read reviews, read plays, and write what you think. You're on your own for awhile. Learn something."

Among the plays I chose to read was *The Connection* by Jack Gelber, a young playwright, only twenty-seven years old. The play horrified me. Set in a New York apartment, a group of heroin addicts were waiting for their fix. The play worked its way into my skin, haunted me. In fact, *The Connection* might have been one of the most important reasons I steered clear of drugs. It left me repulsed, terrified, and nauseated.

The first performance of the play was on July 15, 1959. By the Living Theatre. Under the tutelage of charismatic Julian Beck. To learn that Julian Beck and some of the people who slept in the rooms across the hall from me at Lilli's may have been the actors in the play made me reel. How could I have been so completely dismissive of them? Immediately, I hounded Lilli with questions.

I knew that Beck was drawn to *The Connection* because Gelber developed his characters with no regard to race. This indifference to color was revolutionary. *The Connection* was probably the first American play ever in which color was incidental. I knew that the Living Theatre, besides being committed to racial equality, was also committed to bringing theatre — and their political agenda — to the people. Not just to the sophisticated, educated upper class, but to everyone. They had come to Brazil, said Lilli, to unshackle the thousands of people dwelling in the slums of Rio, São Paulo, and Minas Gerais. They would make the favelados into not just their audience, but their stars. And into activists who would break down class barriers.

ELIZABETH BISHOP

"YOU CANNOT LEAVE BRAZIL without celebrating Easter in Ouro Prêto," Vera had said. "While you're there, you should visit Dona Elisabetchy. She will be lonely during the holidays, and I'm certain she will appreciate speaking English," Vera had said.

"Dona Elisabetchy?" I asked.

"An American poet who keeps a house in Ouro Prêto. We call her E lis a bet chee, but, to you, in English, she is Miss Elizabeth. Elizabeth Bishop. Perhaps, you have heard of her? She is very well known in the States."

"Heard of her?" I was trembling. I could remember sitting on the quad under the cherry trees at the University of Washington, picking apart the metaphors and similes in "The Fish" with my poetry class, senior year. I could remember images, even exact lines, of the poem. Meeting the poet—someone I had studied—was too good to be true.

"I'll arrange a meeting. She has never learned Portuguese very well and welcomes speaking in English. And she has had such sadness recently. A visit with Americans would be good."

I couldn't believe it. Elizabeth Bishop. Author of "The Fish." A famous poet. Actually visiting her in her own home. What if she and I could have some sort of understanding…a connection…after all, I, an island girl, knew a little about fish…

I envisioned her as wise and wonderful, gentle and grandmotherly. Graying hair. Soft eyes. I would hang on her every word. She would ask to see my poems…she would be magnanimous, of course, and easily recognize my poetic longings…she would volunteer to help me on my way…she would be my mentor…maybe…

SHORTLY BEFORE NOON, LILLI, Karen, and I set off for our meeting with Elizabeth Bishop. We walked down steep sidewalks, edged by walls of piled stones covered in tangles of vines, to the house of "Dona Elisabetchy," Rua Quintiliana 546. We stopped at the door, a huge wooden door—easily nine-feet tall—that looked as if it had come from a church or a castle. Painted bright yellow, it was set in a frame painted blue. Nailed high on the wall was an oval sign, white enamel on metal, with blue lettering spelling "Casa Mariana."

We didn't knock; Lilli just opened the door, and we followed her in. She led us into a room that looked out over the lush green hills and down upon the valleys strewn with red-tiled roofs. Then she said goodbye and left. Karen didn't say a word, but I could tell that she felt as strange as I felt. What were we supposed to do? Where was Elizabeth?

The furniture in the room was eclectic—small tables with fussy turned-wood legs placed next to rustic tables made from split-open tree trunks. Books were stacked here and there, a few trinkets, some framed drawings and primitive watercolors on the walls. A rocking chair. There was a black wood-burning stove, and, through an open door, we could see a cabinet painted with colors like cinnabar and mustard.

On the ceiling were exposed rafters. And hanging from them were several wooden marionettes — their heads flopped to the side as if their necks were broken. The windows were uncurtained, and the shutters were wide open. A breeze touched the strings of the puppets, and they knocked together, but they never once tangled. Their painted eyes seemed to loll in the sockets, and their wet-like red mouths, carnival creepy, gaped in hysterical smiles. One wore a blue suit and a couple of others wore blue dresses; colored ribbons curled from their wrists and ankles.

The ceiling itself was unusual — white and textured. Woven like the uneven weft and warp of a hand-made basket. If counting holes in ceiling tiles helped pass time in a doctor's office, maybe following the wood strips in Elizabeth's ceiling could do the same. In and out, in and out, I followed the narrow strips of wood from the east wall to west, and back again.

Then, just as we were about to give up and leave, she arrived — above us on the landing, a staggering shape of blue velvet dressing gown and electric hair. Her eyes were haunted, startled from sleep. Karen and I held our breath, speechless. Elizabeth looked frightened. And, to us, she was frightening. She shook her head awake, listed toward the wall, and turned back into the room from which she'd come. For a split second, I felt caught in a still life. Blue marionettes. Blue Elizabeth. Out the paned windows, blue sky. Somewhere in the room, a bowl of tangerines against a white wall. A composition in blue with orange. An unsettling tension.

The door closed, and we heard the lock turn. Karen and I didn't know what to do. We sat, afraid to speak, crossing and uncrossing our knees, fidgeting with our hands, afraid to stay, afraid to leave. Some time later — it seemed like forever — Elizabeth reappeared. Her gray hair was tamped down and pushed back, and, when she descended the stairs, she touched the railing only lightly. She looked calmed, but suspicious. Maybe a little embarrassed. The wild-eyed deer-in-the-headlights woman, however, had disappeared, replaced by someone a bit severe, someone contained, with little warmth.

She was short and dressed in gray pants. That the winner of the 1970 National Book Award and the 1956 Pulitzer Prize was wearing pants—on Easter Sunday yet—made an impression on me. The wearing of pants was still a controversial issue at the American School. And in other places as well. It had been only three years since women were allowed to wear pants on campus at the University of Washington without causing a stir.

Elizabeth pulled a chair over and sat facing us, but she was not really looking at us. Without saying a word, she fidgeted with a box of cigarettes and a box of matches, placing the matches on top of the cigarettes, then removing them and holding them. Her hands were shaking. Finally, she pulled a cigarette from the box, put it in her mouth, lit it, and set both boxes next to a ceramic ashtray on the coffee table, close to the bowl of tangerines.

I didn't know what to do or what to say. I kept hoping Karen would speak, but she said nothing. Should we address her as Elizabeth or as Miss Bishop, I wondered. Finally, somewhat awkwardly, I made reference to Vera and to Lilli and then introduced Karen and myself to her. She nodded, but made no comment, offering no indication that she had any idea why we were in her house. Next, quickly running out of insignificant small talk and fumbling for a topic, I asked about the enamel plaque by the door. Had she named the house, or had it been named Casa Mariana by previous owners?

At last, with hardly any inflection at all, she spoke. "I named the house," she said, "for two reasons. First, I named the house to honor Marianne Moore, my mentor. I owe so much to Marianne. Had it not been for her, I might have become a doctor instead of a poet. Marianne taught me to observe. Observation is the key. She and Gerard Manley Hopkins, the priest poet—you know him, don't you?—are the finest observers ever."

Yes, I nodded, I had read Hopkins; I knew about sprung rhythm. "It was Marianne who convinced me that I could write. And second, I named the house for Mariana, the town."

The day before, we had followed Lilli's advice and traveled twelve kilometers to Mariana to see the reenactment of the crucifixion. We had watched a real-life Christ, nearly naked and bleeding, drag his hand-hewn crucifix to the town square, uphill and down. He was followed by a crowd of costumed in-character actors; some taunted and jeered at him while others moaned and cried. Wherever in Mariana the three of us went, we smelled sage, lavender, and violets, but we saw no herbs, no tiny purple flowers. We had no idea why the town smelled like plants, but the scent was wonderful.

At dawn today, Christ's stand-in would have been tied to the crossbeam and left to hang for hours as the townsfolk carried out the crucifixion. Not in Mariana, but in other towns and villages, we were told, the man chosen to be Christ was actually nailed to the cross.

Because it was becoming more and more apparent that Elizabeth was not going to lead the conversation, I asked her a few more questions. She answered dutifully, smoke curling out of her nostrils and her mouth. All of my fantasies about her were going up in smoke, too. She wasn't interested in me or my poems or much of anything else. Trying so hard to make conversation with her was painful, and I could feel a headache coming on, but I kept trying.

I asked her about the unusual ceilings of the house, and she seemed to perk up. "An old man, an ancient old man," she said, "sat on the floor for weeks and weeks and wove the ceilings out of fine split bamboo. Then we painted them white. My ceilings are exactly like those you would have seen here in the 18th century. Actually…maybe you'd be interested…yes, there is something else you might like to see."

Karen and I followed her, wondering what she intended to show us. The house was large, five bedrooms, with several stories—I don't know how many—clamped to the mountainside, with balconies overlooking pockets of buildings and deep valleys. As we followed her down a hallway, I peeked into other rooms, noticing paintings and books, and the same eclectic combination of furniture we'd seen in the room where we had started. I saw that she kept her dishes and glasses in an old pharmacy cabinet, and antique lamps were scattered throughout the house. She said that before she took over the house, cats, ducks, and chickens had free run of the place.

"The old man who lived here before me—he was out of his mind—kept burros in the basement. You can imagine the horrible mess."

As we walked, she mentioned some of the renovations that had been made to the house and grumbled about the lack of good help. "You can't believe how difficult it is to find dependable people here. Brazilians are like children. They don't show up when they say they're going to—tomorrow means a month—they steal me blind, they…I think I've had six plumbers, and none of them know what they're doing. What should take an hour takes a week. It's enough to drive a person…I really want to sell this house."

I was uncomfortable hearing her tirade, wishing that she'd stop complaining. Brazilians charmed and delighted me, and, in my fantasy, I wanted her to love them, too. I didn't want her to be like so many of the Americans I'd met at the embassy—who, disrespectfully, called Brazilians "Brazis" and thought they were ignorant.

In what seemed to be a sitting room, she stopped and nodded for us to come closer. She pointed to a wall and smiled; her eyes, for the first time, seemed alive. Screwed to the wall, maybe 10" × 12", was a glass plate. "For centuries, this house has been added onto and added onto," she said. "This is one of the oldest walls of the original house. Look in."

Behind the glass were layers and layers of boards and panels, posts, and paint. I could see thick heavy beams attached to one another by leather thongs. It was a maze of straw, stucco, cording, and wood. Now, standing in front of the wall, Elizabeth seemed to be growing.

No longer slumped with her head cast down, she was turning professorial, in charge and capable. In minute detail, like a college lecturer, she pointed out to us every individual bit of building material and explained in depth its composition and function.

I began to realize that although Elizabeth had terrified me at first, I was beginning to feel a little more comfortable with her — and her with me. It even seemed that I was getting some of what I'd hoped for — she was teaching me something about how to look and how to see, serving up a treatise on the power of detail. To really see, I told myself, I must look up, down, around, and especially in. I must go deep beneath the surface to know things, and there is so much to observe and so much to discover.

"I would like you to see something else, if you have time," Elizabeth said. "And I can point out some of the local attractions as we go."

We stepped out onto the street, and I saw that from some vantage point inside or outside of Casa Mariana, at least seven of the thirteen cathedrals of Ouro Prêto were visible. Elizabeth pointed to the churches and named each one. Many of the churches, she told us, housed statuary and stonework created by Aleijadinho, the Little Cripple.

We knew the story from Fodor and other travel books, but I wanted to hear it again, in her words. During the time of Tiradentes and the eighteenth-century conspiracy, she said, Aleijadinho, Antonio Francisco Lisboa, sculpted religious forms from the soapstone found in the area. "Such lovely stone. Green and gray, flecked with darks and lights." Born in 1730 to a respected Portuguese architect and a black slave named Izabel in Vila Rica, Aleijadinho, by age fourteen, was already something of a master carver of wood and stone.

"The sculptures are crude," she said, "but very powerful, very dramatic against the white church with bright blue doors and against the green hills."

Elizabeth led us some distance, and I felt as if we were going in circles. We moved back and forth into the shade of pastel-colored shops alongside white-walled residences then out again into the sunlight. It seemed somehow as if we were close to Lilli's. She spoke of the buildings and of the people who lived in them — one whose rosy-faced child she adored, another who was her favorite taxi driver, someone who grew remarkable pole beans. Eventually we found ourselves on a steep switchback parallel to, but I think, above Casa Mariana.

"Here it is," she said. Before us was a boulder, damp and lichen-covered. Split down the middle was a narrow fissure, and up, out of the crack, twined a frail spindle of leaf and blossom.

"Marvelous, isn't it?" she said. "That a flower can grow right out of rock is certainly a miracle. A metaphor for living."

Just a few steps away, Elizabeth led us through a gate beneath a massive crossbeam overhung with vines. The area, about thirty feet long, was enclosed by a stonewall nearly a yard wide, and the piled stones were overhung with drooping mosses, rock-climbing orchids, and what looked like liverwort. Ferns sent out thick curling fronds, fruit trees — peach, guava, and apple — grew in no particular pattern, and a couple of the tallest avocado trees I'd ever seen soared over us. A small shallow brook wound through the garden, and the lanky stems of bright flowers tumbled onto heaved-up stepping stones. Masses of unpruned laurel and quince pushed against the stone wall, and in one corner, herbs had gone to seed, tangling with overgrown sprawling weeds.

"The secret garden. Come in."

April. This was an autumnal garden. Some plants were still full and lush, flowering profusely; others had wilted or were already dead. I didn't know the names of much of anything, but I saw plants that looked like yarrow and catnip, and some like phlox, columbine, and coral bells. It was a chaotic paradise of neglect and disorder, yet it was wild and wonderful. It reminded me of home, of my mother's garden. For this secret place, Elizabeth, thank you, I thought to myself.

We spent several minutes in the garden. She told us to make a bouquet. As we picked, she turned over an upside down bucket and uncovered a few lengths of string and some newspapers. We wrapped our flowers, and then it was time to leave.

"If you hear of anyone who wants to buy the house, let me know... I'd really like to sell it," Elizabeth said, shaking our hands. "I wish you a safe journey home."

I waved good bye, unaware that the journey to understand Brazil's effect on me was just beginning.

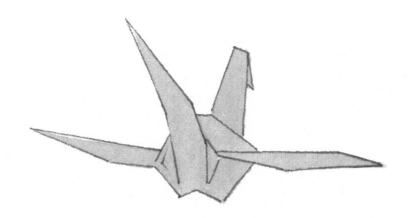

AFTERWARD: BROCTON, ILLINOIS
July 2007

I T HAS BEEN THREE months to the day since my mom died. Thankfully, my husband JR, our daughter Jaime, and I were able to get to her in Seattle before she passed away. I can still see us there—the three of us and my brother and my sister—by mom's side, her hand, cool and thin, in Jaime's hand, as if no time has gone by.

Together, we watch the video made—just a short month ago—of our son Marcus, the prince of random acts of kindness, marrying beautiful Erin high on a mountaintop over Berkeley, California. We hold photographs close to her, so she can see her great grandchildren—three-year-old Megan and the eight-month-old twins, Jack and Andy. Andy...who was named for my dad, her husband. The babies are tucked smiling in the arms of Jaime and her husband Jim. Meg mugs for the camera with the squinty eyes and fake stretch-lip grin that three-year-olds make when they're told to smile. All three little ones are blue-eyed—neither of their parents have blue eyes, but my mom does, and I do. Their hair is reddish-gold, and the boys are almost carbon copies of each other.

We tell mom about the most recent movies that have been shot on the street in front of the apartment in Los Angeles where our daughter Ann and her boyfriend Klutch live, laughing because super-stars Robin Williams and Mandy Moore have been sitting on the streetside window sill of their living room for weeks, talking on cell phones, waiting for cues, and I say that a coffee table book of the backsides of movie stars could be a best seller. We tell her how much Ann loves her job in the Research Institute at the Getty, and how excited we are about the next gallery showing of Klutch's sculptures and drawings from his satellite series. Mom was an artist. Even as weak as she is, she smiles.

I wish I could tell her that two days ago, Ann and Klutch were married.

MOM'S PASSING, COMING SO close to the deadline for finishing my Brazil stories, left me feeling sorrowful and troubled. Mourning her, I didn't know how, or if, I could complete the memoir on time. But, after giving myself what Mom would have called "a good talking to," I made the decision to try. Struggling to edit what I had already written and trying to write the final pages, my insides crawled with anxiety and with thoughts either so blocked that they wouldn't come clear, or so nagging that they refused to disappear. But, Tuesday night, July 24th, I was at Jaime's house, rocking Andy to sleep, when I was hit suddenly with the overwhelming compulsion to find mom's journal and read it, page by page. I handed the baby to his mother and drove home.

I had read her journal before, but only parts of it, certain sections that I thought I could read without falling apart; I had put the rest away to read later when I was stronger, more used to her being gone. Tuesday night, I read every word on every page, crying uncontrollably, thankful that I was alone, that my husband was away, that the phone didn't ring, that the room was dark.

The journal is written in her own hand. Words are crossed out, and, sometimes, she has put down three or four spellings for the same word, with a question mark asking "spelling?" She has written side notes in the margins. When I read them, it's as if she's alive on the page, stepping in — sometimes laughing, sometimes serious — to comment on her descriptions and her recollections.

The journal begins, "What goes around comes around. I promised Jaime this Christmas year of 2001 that I would jot down a few unimportant small episodes of my early years of life that loom in my mind. Some events are still painful to recall and they still lodge deep anxiety in the night until reasoning brings the light of day." On the first page, she writes to us, "It's fair to say that being of pure Swedish heritage is an important reason to pray for the sun — with periods of pain, feelings of depression — pure joy comes when the day brings sun."

In March 1970, she came to Rio for the sun — and, also, of course, for me. She gloried in the sun, closing her eyes, putting her face to it. There weren't enough hours in the day or night for me to share everything I loved about Brazil with her, but we bought a watermelon and cracked it open on the street, eating it with our fingers, letting juice run down to our elbows. We went to On the Rocks; she said she couldn't eat because she had only enough room for the view. We went to the feira where she bought armloads of flowers; she couldn't get enough of them. In Washington, flowers are a short summer affair; in Rio there were flowers every day of the year. She tried, in a week, to bring a year's worth into my apartment. We were without vases, so she put them in jars and teacups and coffee pots.

Watching her pull off leaves, measure stems, and shape the bouquets, I missed my home in Anacortes where her gardens were a wild profusion of abundance, masses of color spilling from hanging baskets, huge planters, and the earth itself. I marveled that she was not only an artist with paint, but also an artist with nature.

Mom raised the flowers, and Dad grew the vegetables. Green and purple striped beans grew jungle-thick, overgrowing their poles; artichokes, glaucous green and silvery, presented their stickery globes like gifts; and corn grew as tall as the apple tree leaning into the rows. No one was ever prouder of a tomato or a carrot than my dad.

Before she came to Brazil, except for our boat trips every summer to the Canadian San Juans, Mom had never left the States. Her week in Rio lifted her to a new realization of what she wanted, where she wanted to be, and what she needed to see. After Rio, she and my dad traveled to Europe time after time — trips to Sweden to visit the relatives, trips to Italy to see where dad had been wounded in the war by a hand grenade, the only survivor of his unit. Finland and Russia. They went to China and Japan and spent winters in Maui or Mexico, so mom could have her sun. They drove to Alaska and Nova Scotia and Cabo San Lucas, taking back roads and "long-cuts," in the blue Volkswagen bus.

After a trip, she would thank me, saying it was because of my travels to England to study and to Brazil to teach that she gave herself permission to leave her kitchen and her backyard garden to make the world her home. She told me that she named me right; I was named for her uncle Leo who, at age eight, ran away from Sweden to become a cabin boy on a ship that sailed the globe. That she made the world her home is, I think, the finest legacy she could bestow on all of us who follow her.

When I boarded the plane to Rio in July 1969, Brazil was just a glossy full-color travel poster in my mind. A montage of beaches, bikinis, cable cars to Sugar Loaf, and the statue of Christ the Redeemer looking over the city. In the foreground, a dark-skinned beauty, a hibiscus in her hair, tipping her head to the camera...in the background, a heartthrob of a boy smiling with the most gorgeous white teeth ever.

By the time I boarded the plane in Rio to return to Seattle in July 1971, Brazil was my home, the place where I grew up. The experience that was Brazil was a gift, a surprise package from someone or something unknown, bestowed freely, nothing required in return, no strings attached. In Brazil, each day, hour, minute, and second was among the finest presents I had ever received and ever would receive.

But, it was a gift that had its share of problems and pleasure. I could identify, uncomfortably and compassionately, with Mom's early references in her journal to our Swedish proclivity to feel deep, penetrating pain, as well as intense joy. As I turned through the pages, carefully reading, one story caused me stop. I had to shut my eyes, think back, and remember that I had heard it years ago. After a few minutes, I read it through, from start to finish. At the last phrase, "I hope I have forgiven myself," I felt such sympathy, so much tenderness and sorrow, that, in some unexplainable way, I claimed it as my story, too.

When she had told me the story a long time ago, I was little, and she had spoken slowly, cupping my chin in her hands, lifting my face so that we could look at each other eye to eye. It happened when she was in junior high in Salt Lake City; for her, it was a new school in a new neighborhood. In the journal, she wrote, "The girls in my class were children of politicians and wealth and very much a part of the Mormon hierarchy."

Mom wanted to be like them; she wanted beautiful blond or brunette hair, but she had flyaway red hair and freckles that she hated. An old lady had told her, "If you rise before first light and bathe your face in the morning dew, the freckles will disappear." But they didn't. She had skipped two grades, so she was two years younger than her classmates. Around these girls who were already beginning to look like women, she felt awkward and scared. She longed to fit in, but always, she was on the outside looking in—she wasn't a Mormon.

For Christmas, more than anything, she wanted a Mickey Mouse watch with a leather band. Her mother, widowed, was always struggling to keep the two of them and her own mother housed, fed, and clothed; a house had been lost once because she couldn't make the payments. But, she saved and saved until she could buy the watch.

On the first day back from Christmas break, the girls gathered in

the hallway, excited to tell about their gifts — new outfits, new jew-
elry, new books, and diaries with locks. Every girl, in earnest, tried
to outdo the others. Each of them had a new watch, and one by one,
they pulled back the sleeves of their blouses and turned their wrists
like ballerinas. Their watches were gold, delicate, dainty, some with
diamonds, the kind of watch a grown-up lady would wear.

"I felt such shame. No young lady of any prestige would ever wear an
ugly Mickey Mouse watch," Mom wrote. She unfastened the watch
and slipped it into the pocket of her coat. After school, she hid it in
her dresser drawer.

When she had told me the story a long time ago, tears welled up
in her eyes. Reading it, tears came to mine. "I was ashamed of the
watch. But that shame turned into a much, much deeper shame," she
had said. In her journal, she wrote, "I had become selfish. I had not
accepted a gift that had so much love contained in it. My mother
would have forgiven me, and after all these years, I hope that I have
forgiven myself."

There were times in Brazil that I felt like my mother must have
felt — a little girl embarrassed by an ugly watch. Like her, sometimes I was out of step, not as someone marching to a different drum,
but as someone isolated, not tuned into the interlocking, symbiotic
connections we share with others. Everyone else seemed older and
wiser, more sophisticated. When I was twenty-one, I was sure that
Karen and Ellen, who were five- and six-years older than I, had all
the answers. I assumed that someone thirty or forty, and surely by
fifty, knew what was what.

At twenty-something, I had not yet gained my mother's kind of
maturity to fully understand bone-deep the profound and penetrating regret she felt about hiding her watch. By failing to wear it proud-
ly as a symbol of her mother's enduring love for her, she suffered. By
failing to wear it fearlessly as a symbol of her own individuality, she
felt diminished. By neglecting to tell her mother of her deception,

she was overcome with guilt. Now, I understand. But then, young and naïve, uncertain, I was not yet aware of the deep shame that permeates us when we fail to acknowledge the connection that we all share as humans and when we fail to stand up for what is right, and true, and good.

For years, Mom and Dad belonged to the local Elks Club. On Saturday nights, they would dress up and go for drinks and dinner. I remember one Halloween night when they, and twenty or so of their friends, went to a party at the club. For weeks, mom and the other wives met in our dining room with their sewing machines, needles, and thread. They sewed identical black-and-white-with-red-bills penguin suits for everyone in their group.

On Halloween, we kids, collected at our house with a babysitter, laughed until we nearly peed our pants, watching the flock of penguins waddle out the door and into their cars to head downtown to the club. When they returned hours later, mom said that it was the weirdest experience ever. No one could figure out who was who — husbands couldn't find wives, and wives couldn't find husbands. Only when they spoke did they find their spouses.

On a Saturday night in the late winter, Mom and Dad returned home and announced, "We quit the Elks Club." They said the club was going to hold a hoop shoot, but that African-American boys would not be allowed to compete. There were no black people in our town, but there were blacks in Seattle and Spokane, and Mom and Dad were adamant that those boys should be able to shoot free throws alongside the white boys. Of course, no one in the 50s, not even my own mom and dad, seemed to have noticed that the other girls in our neighborhood and I dribbled and passed and shot baskets for hours on the blacktop behind our garage.

In Rio, one afternoon, a group of us went from school to have a late lunch at the Copacabana Palace Hotel, the most famed of all Rio hotels. A young black man was with us, down from the States for an internship. He was told to enter the hotel from the servants' entrance; it didn't occur to the doorman that a black man would be in our company. We simply explained the situation, laughed it off, and enjoyed our lunch. It didn't register until afterwards when red-hot shame surged into my body and flooded through me that I realized how wrong I was to have eaten there. I was stung that I could lambaste South African racists, and, then, turn right around and fail to defend the dignity of this good man. I never apologized to him.

Although we were developing an awareness of the civil rights of African-Americans in the 50s and 60s, the issue of sexual orientation was another matter entirely. Some of Mom's artist friends were gay, but their homosexuality was hush-hush, never discussed openly. If anyone had asked if there were gays in my high school, or even in the community, the answer would have been a resounding, "Of course not, absolutely not!" Consequently, it was not so peculiar that with Vera and her friends I spent more time worrying about what others might think than attending to what those brilliant women were saying and what valuable life lessons they could impart. Would so-and-so think I was a lesbian? Could I get fired from the school because I knew lesbians? A late bloomer when it came to any kind of adult relationship, I knew very little of sex and love; the sexual liberation of Vera and her friends terrified me.

When I met Elizabeth Bishop, as silly as it seems, I was still of the mind that somebody as old as she — ironically the same age as I am now — should have her life together. I could only quantify our meeting by how I felt — awkward, inept, and plain. That she was unresponsive and distant I could only interpret as my fault. The world, at that time, revolved around me. That I didn't recognize her as a lesbian was most likely the result of my own refusal to believe it. In my self-centeredness, I didn't allow her to be who she really was; certainly, all the signs were there. Similarly, I was dismissive of her alcoholism. To envision her as a mean, staggering drunk was not in my lexicon of who I wanted and needed her to be.

In addition, there was no way for me to comprehend the mess that was her life — I had no previous experience, beyond movies and books, to draw on, no means of plumbing my soul to fish out empathic recognition of her situation. The enormity of despair that Elizabeth must have felt after her lover, Lota de Macedo Soares, killed herself in Elizabeth's New York apartment was an emotion I couldn't touch. The guilt that Elizabeth must have felt because her friends blamed her for Lota's death — she had carried on affairs outside her relationship with Lota, she kept secrets from Lota, and, for years, despite Lota's constant pleas that she stop, she drank and drank until she was falling-down drunk — was nothing I could register.

Looking back, I see that the only order in Elizabeth's life may have come from her poetry. A master of form, she found perfect words and fit them into the line perfectly. She forged the depths of things intellectual, moral, and emotional, and submerged her themes back into the deep, relying on us, her readers, to raise them up and discover their treasures on our own. There is solace in knowing that I can return to her poems any time that I want and that there is much more to her as a person than was apparent when I spent the afternoon with her. Although our meeting, at the time, was troublesome and disappointing, it became an opportunity to look outside myself and my own needs, and to develop and nurture much more than a scrap and a whit of compassion.

So, the pain and the regrets pile up. The day in the favela with Maria Elena and her family and friends was one of the best days of my life, but I never went back. I never knew what happened to her. I wrote in my letters that I loved her children, but I never wrote down their names. I dismissed the Living Theatre troupe because they "didn't look right."

I could list failing after failing, each with its own sorrow and its own hurt. But with age comes maturity, and I can forgive myself for being twenty-something. My mom and her watch will always remind me that we must grow into understanding with every day that we live; we—most of us, anyway—aren't born wise. My life to age twenty-one was nearly hazard-free—safe and protected. My life since, in Brazil particularly, has been a collection plate of experiences. These life lessons—both the bad and the good—I offer up in exuberant celebration.

I am grateful that the joyous memories of Brazil prodigiously outshadow those that were painful. The joyous memories—On the Rocks, Maria Elena, New Year's Eve, Easter in Ouro Prêto—have sustained me, enriched me, and empowered me. And, wonderfully, there are hundreds more memories, remembered, but as yet unwritten. The appreciation—the reverence—I feel for the country and its people is without limit.

I came home to America, but I have kept Brazil, my home away from home—Brasil with an s—cradled in my heart.

ALL PROFITS FROM *A Thousand Cranes* support the work of the War Writers' Campaign. The organization's mission is to promote social change surrounding veterans issues through written awareness. As a nonprofit organization and independent publisher, The Campaign aims to nurture veteran and family member storytelling while supporting transformative programs. The War Writers' Campaign depends on the generosity of individuals and revenue generated by sales of the books that it publishes. Each of its publications represent the voices of the writers' military, veteran, and family member community, while giving back to future generations.

47643464R00116

Made in the USA
Lexington, KY
11 December 2015